EXPLORING
THE P   AY

Alan Charles

COUNTRYSIDE BOOKS
NEWBURY, BERKSHIRE

Also by Alan Charles
EXPLORING THE RIDGEWAY

First Published 1990
© Alan Charles 1990

COUNTRYSIDE BOOKS
3, Catherine Road
Newbury, Berkshire

ISBN 1 85306 080 1

Cover Photograph of the Pilgrims' Way near Wrotham
taken by the author
Sketch maps by the author
Line drawings by Leonard J Hayes RIBA
& Richard M Ridlington BA, RIBA

Produced through MRM Associates Ltd., Reading
Typeset by Acorn Bookwork, Salisbury
Printed in England by JW Arrowsmith Ltd., Bristol

Contents

The Pilgrims' Way

'That road, in its winding course from Winchester to Canterbury, through Hampshire, Surrey and Kent, sums up all qualities of roads except those of the straight highway. It is a cart-way from farm to farm; or a footpath only, or a sheaf of half a dozen footpaths worn side by side; or, no longer needed except by the curious, it is buried under nettle and burdock and barricaded by thorns and traveller's joy and bryony bines; it has been converted into a white country road for a few miles of its length, until an ascent over the Downs or a descent into the valley has to be made, and then once more it is left to footsteps upon grass and bird's foot trefoil or to rude wheels over flints. Sometimes it is hidden among untended hazels or among chalk banks topped with beech and yew, and the kestrel plucks the chaffinch there undisturbed. Or it goes free and hedgeless, like a long balcony half-way up the Downs, and unespied it beholds half the South Country between ash tree boles. Church and inn and farm and cottage and tramp's fire it passes like a wandering wraith of a road.'

EDWARD THOMAS
The South Country

MAP SYMBOLS

Forward route along a path or track.	— → — — → —
Forward route along a road.	——→———
Return route along a path or track.	· · · · ← · · ←·.,
Return route along a road.	←———————
Pilgrims' Way – Conjectured or with no public access.	//////////////

Other paths and tracks.	· · · · · · · · ·	Stile	→ –∎→ —
North Downs Way.	· · · *NDW* · · · ·	Steep hill	—→→ —
River.	*R.WEY*	Railway	—·—·—o—·—·—
Fence or hedge	—·—·—·—·—·—	Electricity power line.	—×——×—
Church.	+	House or other building.	∎
Lake.	⬭	Town or village.	▰
Trees or woodland.	♣ ♣	Start of circular walk.	**S**

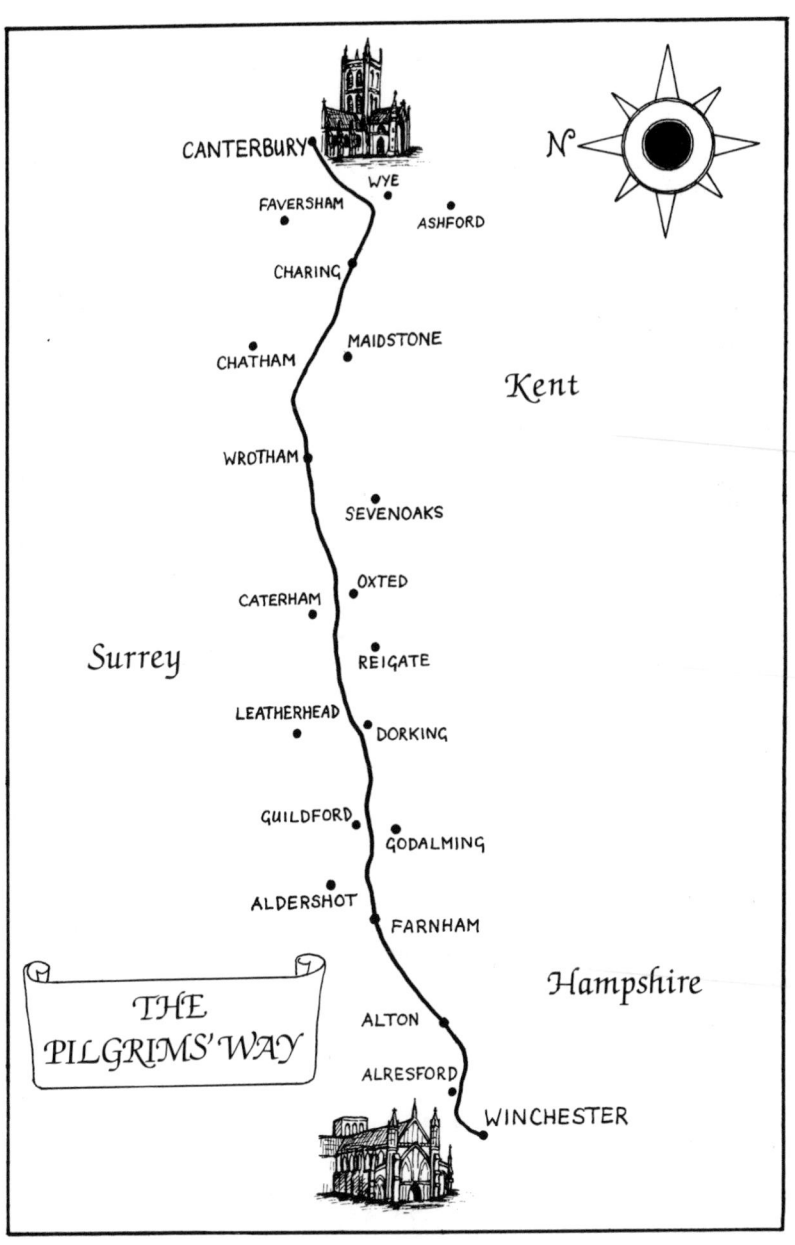

CANTERBURY

WYE

FAVERSHAM

ASHFORD

CHARING

MAIDSTONE

CHATHAM

Kent

WROTHAM

SEVENOAKS

OXTED

CATERHAM

REIGATE

Surrey

LEATHERHEAD

DORKING

GUILDFORD

GODALMING

ALDERSHOT

FARNHAM

Hampshire

THE
PILGRIMS' WAY

ALTON

ALRESFORD

WINCHESTER

N

Introduction

At the start of its 130 mile journey to Canterbury, the Pilgrims' Way is escorted northwards out of Winchester by that most beautiful of Hampshire rivers, the Itchen.

At Headbourne Worthy the Itchen turns eastward on its way to meet the river Alre at Alresford. The Pilgrims' Way goes with it, aiming all the while for the escarpment of the North Downs, heralded by the Hog's Back ridge west of Farnham.

Having reached the North Downs the Pilgrims' Way attempts the easiest route: high enough to avoid damp soils below the 'spring line' (that is where spring water flows from beneath the chalk), yet not so high as to involve rigorous ascents. At least that is the theory – and that is the principle that would have guided ancient man as he made his way along these hills.

The reality is different, however. There are deep combes to negotiate, steep escarpments to traverse, wide river valleys to cross. To our ancestors these features were a hindrance; today they add to our pleasure. The combes open up magnificent views, revealing the escarpment in prospect and in retrospect. The steep south-facing slopes capture the full benificence of the sun and, where the ground is preserved and unmolested, bring forth all the beauty of chalk grass-land shrubs and flowers, and the butterflies and insects that live by them. The north–south flowing rivers – the Wey, the Mole, the Darent, the Medway and the Stour – divide up the landscape and, far from being obstacles in our path, give variety and interest to the scene.

The landscape is further enhanced by all the delightful towns and villages to be seen on, or close to, the Pilgrims' Way. They follow the rivers Itchen and Wey in Hampshire, they nestle below the southern slopes of the downs in Surrey and in Kent.

Looking further afield from these chalk uplands we see the vast expanse of the Weald of Sussex and Kent, which, in spite of all the intrusions of modern man, appears amply garnished with woodlands and green fields. And focusing our eyes more distantly we see, here and there, the grey silhouette of the South Downs terminating the southern skyline.

I have divided the route of the Pilgrims' Way into 19 manageable walks, each corresponding to a chapter and ranging in distance from 5 to 12 miles. These distances are from centre to centre (village or town) and include paths or roads linking the centres with the Pilgrims' Way. Add all these together and you have a total of 145 miles to cover!

Most of the 19 chapters include a circular walk incorporating a section of the Pilgrims' Way and linked to a return route described separately. These circular walks vary in length from 2½ miles to 8½ miles and include as many of the 'best bits' of the Pilgrims' Way as possible. Some of these walks start at or near railway stations (usually coinciding with the beginning of a chapter), and details of car parking near the start of the walk are given.

For the benefit of those walking the Pilgrims' Way on a day-out basis, each chapter, with one exception, includes suggestions for returning to the starting point by public transport.

The Pilgrims' Way, or its nearest practicable alternative, is also described as a continuous route from Winchester to Canterbury, each chapter being linked to the next at the appropriate point in the text. For example, those not ending their first day at Alresford are directed from a point near the end of the first chapter to the point marked (3) near the start of the second. The total distance of the Pilgrims' Way walked in this fashion (what I call the 'through route') is 131 miles.

Where the Pilgrims' Way coincides with long stretches of busy road, alternative parallel paths are followed – for example along the A31 from Alton to Farnham. All the routes described are along public rights-of-way or permissive paths. An example of the latter is the path alongside Chilham Lake. This is owned by the Mid-Kent Water Company who have kindly allowed public access during daylight hours – which to most of us would not be a problem!

For the return routes I have been careful to choose, as far as is possible, only those paths and tracks which are clearly marked and easy to follow, including parts of the well used North Downs Way. Farming interests have in many places taken their toll of the footpath network, and you will notice that many paths, although present on the map, no longer appear on the ground. Rather than immerse you in difficult navigational problems (and risk your criticism!) I have mostly avoided such 'paths' in favour of quiet country lanes.

The sketch maps are intended as a rough guide to the route covered by each chapter, with sufficient information to enable the route to be transferred to more detailed maps. Unfortunately, no less than six 1:50,000 scale Ordnance Survey maps are required to cover the entire route. These are numbered 179, and 185 to 189. This is an expensive undertaking, but a valuable investment that will last for many years.

Less expensive is a compass, but a valuable investment also, and very useful when you are lost! Here and there in the text I have given bearings to enable you to identify places of interest and to direct your feet if the path ahead is not entirely clear or adequately waymarked.

As mentioned elsewhere, the North Downs Way often follows the line of the Pilgrims' Way. This can be quite useful, since the North Downs Way is clearly marked with the Countryside Commission's acorn symbol on concrete plinths, wooden posts, stiles etc. But when the two routes part company, as they often do, it is only too easy to get 'hooked' on the acorns and lose the Pilgrims' Way. So do please keep one eye on the text!

Where some major doubt or controversy exists regarding the route of the Pilgrims' Way, the points at issue are examined under Historical Notes. Where a choice exists I have inclined towards those routes marked on the wayside or on the Ordnance Survey maps as 'The Pilgrims' Way'. This is not an ideal procedure since these indicators are not always without the possibility of error. However, it does go some way in preventing confusion when comparing the directions given in this book with official signposts and maps.

In the preparation for this book I am indebted first and foremost to my daughter Gillian who made such a good job of the typing; not an enviable task! To the Public Paths Officers of Hampshire, Surrey and Kent, who so patiently conducted me through their maps. To Richard Ridlington and Len Hayes for their excellent line drawings. To Dennis Turner for his enthusiastic help, and to the many correspondents who provided information. Thank you one and all.

Alan Charles
March 1990

A Short History of the Pilgrims' Way

Where the six great highlands of Southern England converge on Salisbury Plain, there came an ancient yet sophisticated people, paying homage to the shrines of Stonehenge and Avebury. They came from south-east England and from the Continent. They brought with them amber from the Baltic, faience beads from Egypt. They took away valuable metals – tin, copper, and gold – from the West Country and from Ireland.

They followed the clear line of the North Downs as far as Farnham in Hampshire, and as the ridge melted away their feet marked out a route that would become known as the Harroway, taking them to Salisbury Plain and beyond.

It is said that these ancient people often crossed from the Continent by way of the Straits of Dover. In truth the landfall would be determined by the weather and the state of the sea and the tide. In the course of time a multiplicity of crossings would be established. These would ultimately give rise to a number of important harbours – Lympne, Folkestone, Dover, Sandwich, Richborough, Ramsgate, Reculver.

Once on terra firma, the coming together of these routes would be a likely outcome, a focal point that would be of considerable value to those coming and going on the Old Road – for commerce, for exchange of news, for sociability and, when the need arose, for communal defence.

Canterbury has this focal point, this 'inland gathering place', established since very early times.

Winchester can claim equally valuable credentials: sited on the river Itchen and receiving traffic from a number of natural harbours, from Lymington in the west, to Chichester in the east. Although the crossing from the Continent is much wider here than at the Straits of Dover, on clear days the sight of land is lost for only a fraction of the journey thanks to the high promontory of St Catherine's Down on the Isle of Wight and Barfleur Hill on the Normandy Peninsula.

Winchester also became an important link with the hinterland, a launching-pad for the highways of Wessex. One such highway followed the course of the river Itchen and made its acquaintance with the Harroway at Farnham.

And so we have our Canterbury and our Winchester, each owing its existence to the sea, each linked to the other by a great highway –

the Old Road – a road formed by the feet of men and animals centuries before the Age of Pilgrimage.

Winchester entered a peak in its popularity during the 300 years that followed the death of one of its most loved and respected bishops, Swithun. Tutor of Alfred (later to become one of England's greatest kings), advocate of the poor and the sick, this humble man was remembered long after his death, so much so that pilgrims travelled from many parts of England and the Continent to his shrine at Winchester. Today Swithun is perhaps better known for his influence on the weather: if it rains on St Swithun's Day it will continue thus for 40 days!

It was 308 years after Swithun's death – on 29th December 1170 – that Archbishop Thomas Becket was murdered in Canterbury Cathedral. In contrast to Swithun, Becket was an intriguing mixture of humility and arrogance, of kindness and intolerance.

As a young man Becket was given a post in the Archbishop of Canterbury's household but in 1154 he was appointed Chancellor to King Henry II. On becoming Archbishop of Canterbury in 1162 Becket changed his allegiance from the Crown to the Church, resulting in bitter conflict with King Henry. The King's desire to be rid of this thorn in his flesh led to four of his knights making their way to Canterbury and hacking Becket down within the cathedral, setting in motion a new era in the history of the Church. The whole of Christendom was appalled: the former Chancellor and Primate of all England murdered in cold blood, and in a holy place!

With Becket's martyrdom, Winchester went into decline in favour of Canterbury as a place of pilgrimage, St Swithun's tomb losing its pre-eminence to Becket's. And with reports that miracles were being performed at Becket's tomb, Canterbury drew people like a magnet. Many travelled to Canterbury from London along the route of Chaucer's 29 pilgrims. Many came from Winchester along the Old Road, some having entered the country at Southampton. From such simple beginnings the act of pilgrimage evolved into a national industry.

Every church was required to have its holy relics – old bones, shreds of garments, fragments of vessels, etc, through which the pious beholder, by some mysterious process, would receive a cure for his ills, the remission of his sins, or the satisfaction of worldly ambitions. There seemed to be no limit to which the gullible would go: anything which had the remotest connection with a saint or with our Lord himself would receive a pilgrim's veneration. This continued until the Dissolution of the Monasteries during the reign of Henry VIII.

Over the centuries that followed, parts of the Old Road from Winchester to Canterbury became main highways (our 'A' roads of today) and part evolved into the present (and pleasant!) country lanes. Much of it remained exactly as it has always been – a track or greenway along the side of the escarpment; and some of it disappeared altogether. In a number of places the Old Road was enclosed within great estates – at Gatton, Titsey, Chevening, Eastwell, Chilham, and perhaps Albury.

It was not until the 18th century that maps began to appear with parts of the Old Road labelled as the Pilgrims' Way or Road. The first was in 1769 with the map of Andrews and Drewy, followed by a map published by Hasted in 1778–9. In the 1860s officers of the Ordnance Survey extended this practice and added authority and antiquity in the process.

Numerous writers have since deliberated on the route of the Pilgrims' Way through the counties of Hampshire, Surrey and Kent, often basing their researches on these early maps. Foremost among them was Hilaire Belloc and Julia Cartwright. Belloc set down his theories and chronicled his explorations in a book entitled *The Old Road*, published in 1904. This has become an important work of reference ever since, as has Julia Cartwright's attractively illustrated volume of 1895, *The Pilgrims' Way from Winchester to Canterbury*.

In recent years the North Downs Way long-distance path has come into being, and roughly follows the line of the Pilgrims' Way, starting at Farnham and continuing to Folkstone and Dover. In attempting to avoid tarmac surfaces and low-lying routes, the North Downs Way excludes some delightful country lanes and easy-going paths, and exchanges these for more circuitous paths, sometimes on more difficult terrain. It offers some fine views however, but at a price!

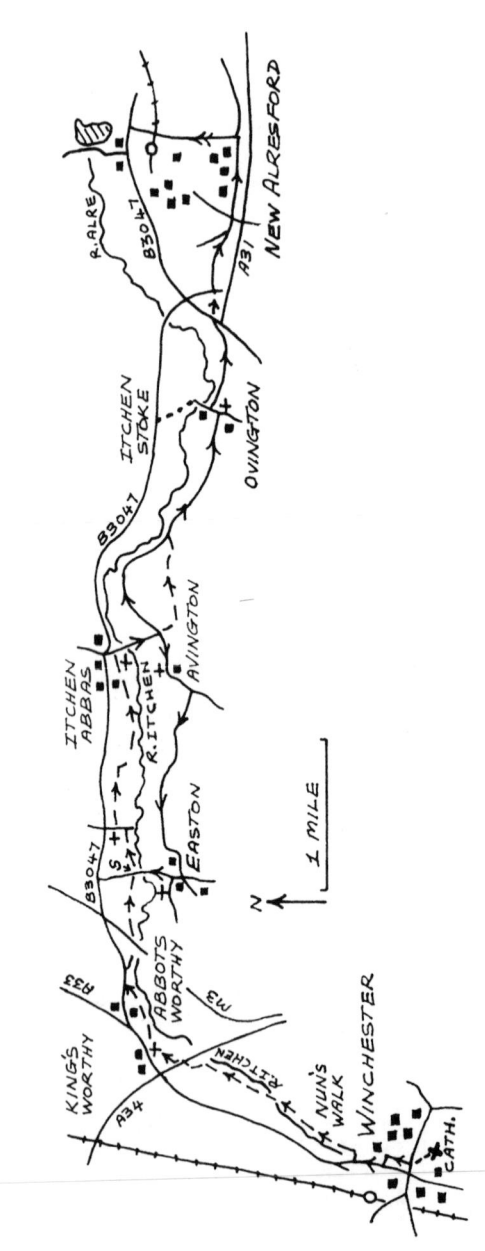

Winchester to
New Alresford

Introduction: Almost the whole of this first walk is spent within close range of the lovely river Itchen, firstly north along Nun's Walk to King's Worthy church, then west along riverside meadows through a string of delightful villages, finally approaching New Alresford from Tichborne Down in the south.

The circular walk takes in the best of these villages, from Easton to Itchen Abbas, returning through Avington along quiet country lanes.

Circular Walk: Easton – Itchen Abbas – Avington – Easton
The walk is 4 miles (6.4 km) and starts at **(1)** on page 15, ¼ mile north of Easton by the river Itchen (grid reference 512325). There is parking available by the roadside at the starting point of the walk.

Pilgrims' Route: Winchester to New Alresford
The walk is 9½ miles (15.3 km) and begins at the Cathedral. There are ample car parks in the city, and roadside parking is possible in Saxon Road near the start of the walk.

To return to Winchester by public transport buses run ½ hourly Mon–Sat (214/215) and 2 hourly on Sunday (453). Classic Buses also run a service from Alresford Station on summer weekends.

The Walk: The true place to commence this 'pilgrimage' is Winchester Cathedral. From the West Door a tree-lined path runs north-west across the Cathedral precincts to the City Museum. From the museum go under the Pentice Arch and into High Street beside the 15th century City Cross. Turn left, then first right into St Peter's Street (more a footway than a street). Before crossing St George's Street spare a few moments at the sight of a 'vanished' medieval church. Excavated in 1956 the site revealed, in addition to the church, evidence of Roman and Norman building work. An adjacent wall-poster tells all.

Cross St George's Street to fully fledged St Peter's Street and go past the Royal Hotel (once a convent) to North Walls. Turn left, then right into Hyde Street. At the crossing a plaque marks the site of the North Gate, demolished in 1756.

Go along Hyde Street and right into King Alfred Place. Here stands the one remaining part of Hyde Abbey of AD 1110, opposite the church of St Bartholomew. There is just a faint chance that the simple gravestone (the one marked with a small cross) outside the west end of the church covers the final resting place of (or more correctly – part of) the Great King Alfred. Read the whole fascinating story in a leaflet obtainable from the church.

Turn left into Saxon Road just beyond the church and go along this to Nun's Road on the right. Cross the bridge in Nun's Road and turn left immediately onto a riverside path – Nun's Walk. This runs alongside a sports field and crosses a drive. The next concrete bridge but one will take you to the left bank of the river by an entrance to Chalkdell Cottage. Well penned-in dogs express their resentment here, in old stables-cum-kennels.

Soon there are fields left and right while you are accompanied by another branch of the river; eventually recrossing the river by means of a large sheet of metal with an equally large pipe alongside – adequate and official! Next there is a more considerable branch of the river on your right as you approach a stile. Some non-conformists have crashed through the hedge to the A34, but you should turn left along a path parallel to the road.

At the end of that path turn right through two tunnels in succession, then left and parallel to the road again. When the path emerges at an industrial site turn right across the tarmac precinct and aim for a path to the left of a rank of black poplar trees – as directed by footpath signposts. You will pass a transformer on your right and car parks left and right. King's Worthy church soon comes into view, as does a very welcome churchyard seat which is a delight when bathed in the warm summer sun.

Leave the churchyard at its eastern end, passing a five-sided vestry, and turn right into St Mary's Close by the Old Post Office. I am told that this was the first post office in Britain! Go straight on along St Mary's Close, between garages old and new (not left to Ambury) and through a tiny orchard to the A33. Cross the A33 very carefully to a signposted path opposite.

There is a marshy area to the right of the path – a fine place for birds and dragonflies! You are soon led to an iron gate and transferred to the right bank of a stream. This leads you to a drive by Abbotts Worthy Mill. Before crossing to a kissing-gate a short diversion to the right is recommended for a view of the river. Now from that kissing-gate go uphill to a stile at the far left-hand corner of a field, at the end of a long, low farm building. Then aim straight on across the next field to a stile in the furthest corner, at a road.

Go forward in the road to a stile just beyond a house called 'The Worthys'. A path will then take you in a curve along the right-hand edge of a field and under the M3. Beyond the M3 the path turns left then right to follow the border between a cultivated field left and a pasture right, along a line of fenced-in trees.

Keeping straight on you will in due course arrive at the Easton Road, whose church you may have noticed already. Cross the road to a clear path opposite. (1) Those starting the circular route from here should turn right into the path from the lay-by, near the Easton road sign.

It is a pleasant fieldside path now, followed by a perambulation around a goats' paddock and a private garden to the road at Martyr Worthy. Turn left here for the church, or right for an out of this world view of the river. The church has very old, recently restored roof timbers, a Victorian chancel, a dog-tooth arch above the south door and, best of all, a seat in the sun!

Cross the road from the church and go along a rough drive signposted to Itchen Abbas. Passing the village hall on the left go forward to a kissing-gate where the drive turns right, then straight on across a field along a slightly terraced path to the right of more fenced-in trees. This will soon lead you alongside a hedge on the left – enclosing a field on the left – and to another gate. You then have a succession of fields and stiles before being steered half-right along a fenced path to a road at Chilland where there's another view of the river if you divert to the right.

To continue the walk go left in the road for a few yards and join a fenced path on the right. An impressive Georgian-style house, Chilland Place, will be in view on the left as you proceed. A stile will then lead you into a fenced field-edge along the river bank where two stiles on the left should be ignored. Once in the next field (via a gate) you should veer left and uphill to join the right-hand arm of a wire fence leading to a kissing-gate at the far end. You will pass to the right of two large houses before crossing a tree-lined track.

Straight on now, with gardens left and meadows right, and soon by Itchen Abbas church. After you have visited the church (a 'must' for all pilgrims!) turn right in the road from the lychgate and cross a river bridge, followed later by another. Avington Lodge and the entrance to Avington House will be on your right before you reach a T-junction. Turn right here if you are on the circular route and continue from page 17.

To continue the main walk turn left here. Now you are spoilt for choice: either stay in this very nice, quiet road or take to the fields. We will meet up less than a mile along the road – before Yavington Farm Cottage. The 'footpath', a wide track, leaves the road on the right just after the T-junction. Follow it up and left near the top. Then it is absolutely straight on, eventually through a copse and across a field before turning left along the field-edge – all commendably arrowed by 'Landowners welcome caring walkers' waymarks! A stile in the fence on the right will lead you into another field and back to the road.

Before Yavington Mead, a beautiful Georgian house at the end of a drive, you have another choice. Either stay in the road (climbing the hill ahead) or take to the fields again, and enjoy an unforgettable view of the river. For the latter, go along the drive to a stile on the right of Yavington Mead. Keep your head high – it *is* a right-of-way! Then straight on across a field to another stile, and along the left edge of the next field to its far left-hand corner. Turn left in a path under trees for that view of the river (far enough to see the second branch), then about turn in this *same* path to rejoin the road (ie. not back to Yavington Mead).

In due course you will arrive at Ovington opposite flint and brick Lane End Cottage. Turn right for the church, and its accompaniment of attractive cottages. In the churchyard may be seen the arch of an earlier Norman church.

Now go back downhill from the church to the Bush Inn, and before turning right in the road, a few steps ahead to the river footbridge would be well rewarded. It is thought that pilgrims crossed the river here from what is now the B3047 and continued along the route that you will now follow.

With your back to the Bush Inn it is ⅔ mile of Pilgrims' Way road to its meeting with the B3047 link road, firstly beside the river, then under elderly beech trees. Cross the link road slightly left of the A31 roundabout to a bridleway opposite and follow this down (A31 Alresford bypass on your right) to a quiet road-crossing. Then go straight on over a ford and through a watercress farm, soon joining a road coming in from the left. Over the next crossing (B3046) by the Cricketers and parallel to the bypass until the road turns left at Sun Cottage. Go left with the road here (Sun Lane) and follow it through to New Alresford.

For the through route staying on the Pilgrims' Way turn right out of Sun Lane almost immediately into the Bishop's Sutton road, and continue from (3) on page 21.

Returning to Easton from Itchen Abbas: Having turned right at the T-junction beyond Avington Lodge follow the road, with an excellent view of the House, to Avington village, passing the Georgian church on the right (see Historical Notes). The road curves left then right by a terrace of flint and brick houses and what is left of the village well.

Take the first right turn after the village, signposted to Easton and Winchester. There is a hay-barn on the corner here. You will pass Avington Picnic Area on the right quite soon – with another view of Avington House. It is then a simple matter to follow the road one mile to Easton, a delightful village with thatched cottages and tidy gardens.

To complete this circular walk turn right in the village at the T-junction by the Cricketers. Keep straight on and your car should soon be in sight.

Historical Notes

There seems little doubt that the Pilgrims' Way followed the line of the river Itchen northwards to King's Worthy church along Nun's Walk, and not along the modern highway. From Abbots Worthy to Itchen Stoke the Way is one and the same as the B3047; we avoid this by taking an alternative route closer to the river. The Pilgrims' Way probably crossed the river at Itchen Stoke and skirted the southern extremity of New Alresford on dry ground. In this way the confluence of rivers and streams that feed the Itchen to the north of Alresford and the consequent marshy ground, was avoided.

Winchester: The briefest of information sheets from Winchester's Tourist Centre lists no less than 16 'places to visit'. A short walk that takes in some of these and is both pleasant and interesting, starts from the City Bridge. Here a path accompanies the river Itchen southwards, not to be confused with a tributary flowing through the Abbey Gardens – as delightful as this is! The City Mill is behind you as you proceed. This was built in 1744 and now houses the Youth Hostel.

Having followed the river and city wall as far as Wharf Mill, join College Street on the right. A path on the right gives access to Wolvesey Castle (you pay to see!). On the left stands Winchester College, founded in 1382 for 70 'scholars for the church' and now one of the country's leading public schools; also the house where Jane Austen died in 1817. Then through King's Gate and Priory Gate to the beautiful Cheyney Court – once the Bishop of Winchester's Courthouse.

As you head for the Cathedral's West End you will pass the Deanery, recognisable by its three Gothic arches. This originally formed part of the Priory of St Swithun. A little beyond the West End the green is marked with the outline of the Old Minster, demolished in 1093. Notice in particular the stone that identifies St Swithun's burial place.

The present cathedral was 'begun' in 1079 soon after the Norman Conquest. Although the building has been altered time and again over the centuries, it still retains some very early features, including the 'oldest and finest crypt in the country'. It is at this level that the most outstanding work (to my way of thinking) has taken place – in the underpinning of the building with concrete in 1900. Before this could be done a diver was 'sent down' to remove the decaying foundations, which consisted of nothing more than a raft of logs laid on a peat bog!

If you make your way along High Street to the 600 year old Westgate you will be in range of the Great Hall with the famous 'King Arthur's' Round Table and Queen Eleanor's 'fairy tale' garden. At the other end of town St Giles' Viewpoint is where you can see it all – and get away from it all!

Itchen Abbas: A pleasant village hovering on the edge of the Pilgrims' Way (the B3047), and the turning-point for the circular walk. Well known residents of Itchen Abbas have included Charles Kingsley, who wrote part of *The Water Babies* here, and Earl Grey of Earl Grey tea!

The Church of St John the Baptist dates back only to 1863. While we may regret the sweeping away of an earlier Norman Building in making way for the new, the present church, especially inside, is a

18

delight. The human scale of its cruciform pattern generates a homely, meaningful atmosphere. Shaded by a tall yew tree close to the church is the grave of 26 year old John Hughes, a gypsy and the last man in England to be hanged for horse stealing. A sombre note in such an agreeable setting!

Avington Park, in view on the return part of the circular walk, is a 17th century house of simple Palladian style. The State Rooms are open to the public at weekends throughout the summer months (afternoons only). The church, completed in 1771 and 'one of the best preserved Georgian churches in the county' is in the same red brick as the House. Walk thoughtfully over the gravestone pavement as you approach the church. Inside, a framed copy of *Country Life* chronicles the restoration of the church from a state of decay, and a barrel organ boasts 31 hymns and 6 chants!

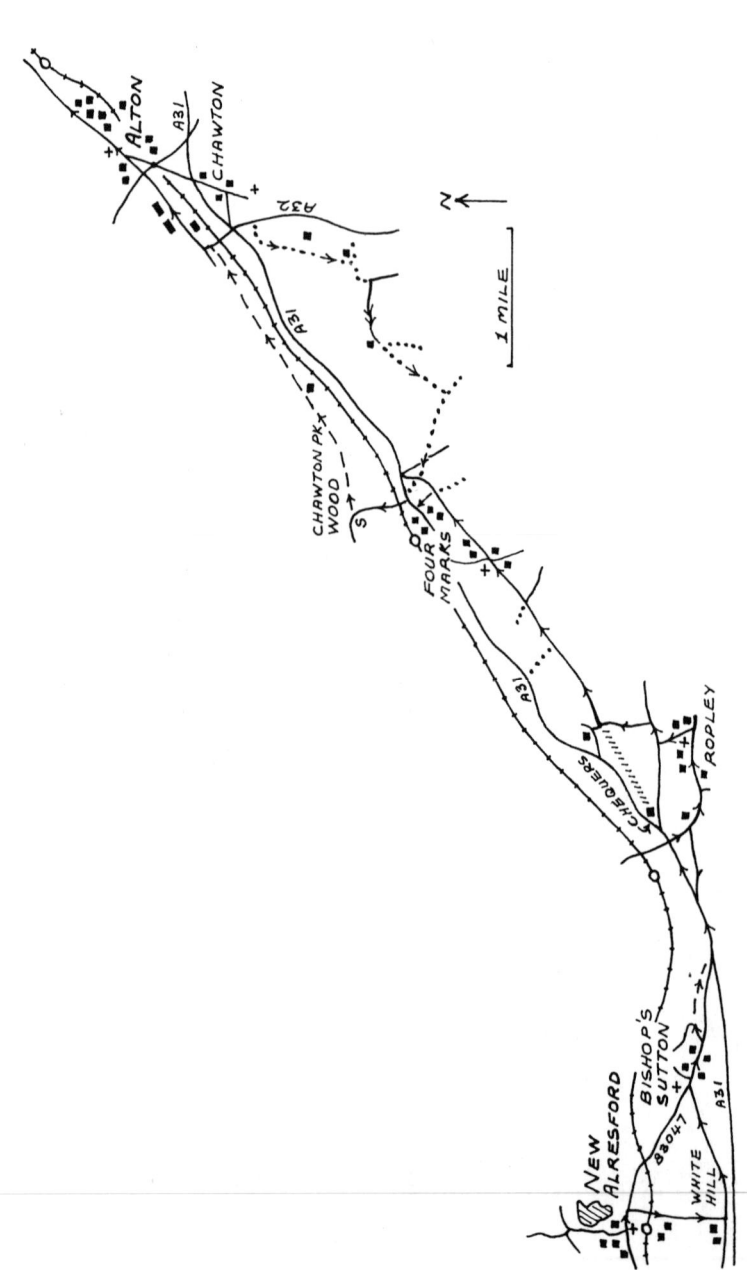

New Alresford
to Alton

Introduction: A day of contrasts: quiet country roads and easy-going field paths, with fine views of the Hampshire countryside; the pretty village of Ropley; wooded Chawton Country Park and the occasional sighting of a steam engine on the Mid-Hants Railway. For the sake of peace and quiet, the Pilgrims' Way is avoided where it becomes the A31 – from Bishop's Sutton to Ropley Dean and from Four Marks to Alton. And as a further concession, you may save yourself 1½ miles of road by taking the 214/215 bus from Alresford to Bishop's Sutton!

The circular walk includes Chawton Park Wood and provides an opportunity to visit Jane Austen's House in its lovely village setting.

Circular Walk: Chawton Park Wood – Chawton – Woodside Farm – Chawton Park Wood
The walk is 6 miles (9.7 km) and starts at **(4)** on page 22, ½ mile north of Four Marks at the Forest Car Park (grid reference 672360).

Pilgrims' Route: New Alresford to Alton
The walk is 12 miles (19.3 km) and begins at East Street. There is parking in Station Road nearby.

To return to New Alresford by public transport, buses run hourly Mon–Sat (214/215) and 2 hourly on Sunday (453). The Mid Hants (Steam) Railway runs March–Oct, but not daily. *Sunday April = 10.15 (Alton*
11.20 →Alton)

The Walk: From Alresford's East Street go along Sun Lane for ⅔ mile to a road junction by Sun Cottage (where Sun Lane turns right). Turn left into the road signposted to Bishop's Sutton. **(3)** This is a one mile piece of the Pilgrims' Way and runs beside Alresford's bypass initially. After that, it is a fairly quiet road to Bishop's Sutton.

21

On arrival at Bishop's Sutton turn right in the B3047 (previously the A31) and third left into Water Lane, next to The Plough. Cross a ford quite soon (not a difficult task!), and when the lane turns left continue forward along a footpath. This passes bungalows on the left and joins a field ahead at a stile. Now it is a simple matter of keeping straight on between fields until you come to a roundabout on the A31. Three cheers to the farmer who has left a good, wide path!

From the roundabout you have one mile of A31 in the Alton direction, almost to The Chequers public house. My apologies for taking you along this busy road! It is, after all, the Pilgrims' Way; and there is a pavement; and there is an opportunity to divert along Station Hill to the Mid-Hants railway depot!

The next part of the Pilgrims' Way (from The Chequers onwards) can no longer be followed, but you can renew contact ¾ mile further on at Manor Farm. To do this turn right into Berry Hill (well before The Chequers) and follow this lane to the pretty village of Ropley. Turn first left after Ropley church, right into Gascoigne Lane at a T-junction, then first left into Court Lane (opposite Bounty House). Now don't go all the way to Manor Farm – except for a closer look at the farmhouse – but turn right 30 yards before it into a quiet lane. This is the Pilgrims' Way once more, which originally extended across the fields behind you – or so they say!

Enjoy this peaceful lane while you may: before long enter Four Marks bungalowland. At the crossroads ahead continue straight on into Blackberry Lane. There is a church near the crossing and also a diminutive water-fountain.

You will pass a shop on the left, then Briar Lane. Turn left after 100 yards into a tarmac path between houses 18a and 20. This will take you to the A31 opposite The Windmill. To the left are shops and a fish and chip restaurant (which I heartily recommend!); also Station Approach leading to another Mid-Hants railway station.

But sooner or later you must go the other way – passing The Windmill on the left, and turning first left into Boyneswood Road, signposted 'Medstead 1½ miles'. The railway is soon crossed (watch for steam trains!) before the road turns left at a parking and picnic area adjacent to Chawton Park Wood. (4)

Leave the road here by turning right – not into the muddy bridle-way but into the picnickers' car park. From the far end of the car park bear right to join a long straight path (again not the bridleway), overlooked by three concrete towers. Once in this path turn neither left nor right until, after one mile, you reach Brick Kiln Farm. Over a stile of sorts here and into the farmyard. Then resume your original direction, but in the farm drive, not the lane coming up from the right.

When the farm drive soon curves right to join a racing circuit, go straight on along a footpath under trees. The path runs deeper into the wood and emerges later to give a fine view of Chawton Park Farm and its deer enclosures on the hillside.

If you are following the circular walk, or wish to visit Jane Austen's house in the delightful village of Chawton, turn right when you meet a road signposted to Winchester (you could also reach Alton that way) and continue from the next paragraph.

For the quickest route to Alton don't turn right but go straight on in the road past a sports centre and a hospital; then along The Butts and into High Street. The hospital was originally built for the wounded of the South African War. In 1908 it became a centre for the care of crippled children under the Lord Mayor Treloar Trust (see page 34). The Butts, a triangular green, was once used for archery practice.

Returning to Four Marks From Chawton: (or visiting Jane Austen's house). Go under the Mid-Hants Railway bridge to the A31 round-about. For Chawton and Jane Austen's house take the second exit. This is a 'must' for all modern pilgrims, if only to promenade through this ancient village and to call in at the teashop! (Then for Alton go through the A31 underpass at the eastern end of the village and straight on.) For the circular walk take the A32 Fareham road (third exit from the roundabout) to a stile 150 yards along on the right at the top of a flight of concrete steps.

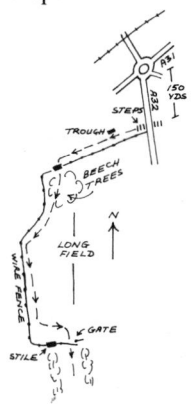

Follow a field edge uphill, passing a cattle trough, towards the right-hand side of a clump of tall beech trees (250 degrees). There is now a waymarked route (yellow arrows), firstly over a stile and under the trees, then along the left side of a wire fence, all the way to an iron gate and stile at the far end of a very large field – with the A32 running parallel well down on your left. The gate leads you into a straight tree-lined track which is all that is left of the Meon Valley Railway! (see Historical Notes).

The track passes under an old railway arch near Southfield Farm, and meets a crossing-track (by a barn) after a further ⅓ mile. Turn right here into the farm track and left with it later, soon joining a tarmaced lane at a turning. Go right in this quiet lane and uphill, soon passing Woodside Farm. Continue straight on in what becomes a track beyond a thatched cottage, ignoring a branch going left into a field quite soon. It is now ½ mile or so just inside woodland – some of it felled – before meeting another track at a T-junction.

Turn right into this track, and when it eventually goes left towards houses, keep straight on beside a wire fence through a beechwood (280 degrees). The well-signposted path runs between gardens, crosses three roads and one track (not all in that order) and meets the A31 at Four Marks. Cross the A31 to Boyneswood Road and go along this to Chawton Park Wood. Home and dry!

Historical Notes

The Pilgrims' Way passes to the south of New Alresford and descends White Hill to Bishop's Sutton. It then coincides with the B3047 and A31 for 2 miles as far as The Chequers at Ropley, ⅓ mile east of Ropley station.

Historians have made much of the next ¾ mile of non-existent Pilgrims' Way! It is thought that the Way headed north-west from the junction of the minor road from Gilbert Street and the A31 – roughly from the garden of The Chequers. An embankment has been observed beside the A31 west of The Chequers, which apparently carried the Pilgrims' Way. I have not seen it, and no amount of author's licence can persuade me that it is there!

It is likely the Pilgrims' Way made its final run into Alton along the line of the present Mid-Hants steam railway and alongside The Butts.

New Alresford: The difficulties of spelling and pronunciation take time to resolve: Alresford in Hampshire; Aylesford in Kent! Adding to the confusion the 'New' in New Alresford means around AD 1200, but Old Alresford has much that is modern! It is a lovely walk down Broad Street, with its avenue of lime trees and its most agreeable houses and shops. Broad Street will lead you into the watery reaches of the river Alre, emphasised by numerous ponds and watercress beds.

Bishop Godfrey de Lucy made an indelible mark on the landscape when he built a huge dam across the Alre as part of his plan to make the river Itchen (into which the Alre flows) navigable as far as Southampton, and as a source of power for a number of watermills. The 200 acre lake that formed, now known as New Alresford Pond and much reduced in size, lies to the right of the road just beyond Broad Street. To the left, a riverside path accompanies the Alre westward. Follow the circuit round: Ladywell Lane – riverside path – The Dean – West Street.

The Mid-Hants Railway, better known as the Watercress Line, runs from Alton British Rail station to New Alresford, a distance of 10 miles. Since the railway runs parallel to the Pilgrims' Way you may have the pleasure – depending on the day and the season (and whether you consider it a pleasure!) – of watching steam-hauled trains plying up and down the valley.

The line was closed by British Rail in 1973 following five years of 'acrimony and dispute' since publication of the closure notice. It was reopened as a preserved railway in 1977, operating between Alresford and Ropley. Two extensions followed: Medstead and Four Marks in 1983, Alton in 1985. Ropley is the most interesting of the Mid-Hants stations since here are sited the 'sheds' where engines and rolling-stock may be viewed.

The Meon Valley Railway: The last train ran along this railway on 5th February 1955, well before Dr Beeching's 'Axe' (so we can't blame him!). The line started life in 1903 and linked Alton to Fareham, a distance of about 24 miles. Like many country lines, its closure resulted from 'a common vicious circle of declining traffic and reduced services'.

Chawton is renowned for its association with Jane Austen, who lived here from 1809 until 1817. Her house is open to the public. Once on the main road to Winchester, Chawton is now a quiet retreat thanks to the bypass, with old cottages, gardens and a teashop. Chawton House and the parish church are located nearby in a peaceful, attractive setting.

Alton to Farnham

Introduction: Since the Pilgrims' Way between Alton and Farnham is almost entirely A31, an alternative and more agreeable route is chosen for today's walk. This is through the attractive villages of Upper and Lower Froyle and across the A31 to join a delightful path beside the river Wey along the border of Alice Holt Forest.

The return part of the circular route also follows the river, but in the opposite direction, passing the magnificent Isington Mill at the half-way point.

Circular Walk: Upper Froyle – Bentley – Isington – Upper Froyle
The walk is 5½ miles (8.6 km) and starts at **(5)** on page 29, by the church at Upper Froyle. There is parking available in Upper Froyle in the wide road linking the A31 (by The Hen and Chickens) with the village.

Pilgrims' Route: Alton to Farnham
The walk is 10½ miles (17 km) and begins at Alton Railway Station.

To return to Alton by public transport, buses run hourly Mon–Sat (214/215) and 2 hourly on Sunday (453) and trains run hourly, ½ hourly in rush hour.

The Walk: From the railway station turn right out of Station Road into Alton's main thoroughfare – Anstey Road at this point. Then go left into Park Close Road opposite Alton Health Centre and join a tarmac path on the right after about 150 yards. This runs parallel to the main road and crosses Lansdowne Road into Chalcrafts. When Chalcrafts turns right continue forward along a path between houses and a football field. Go over the next road and straight on across Anstey Park to a gap in the hedge on the far side, where you will be confronted by a large well-mown school field.

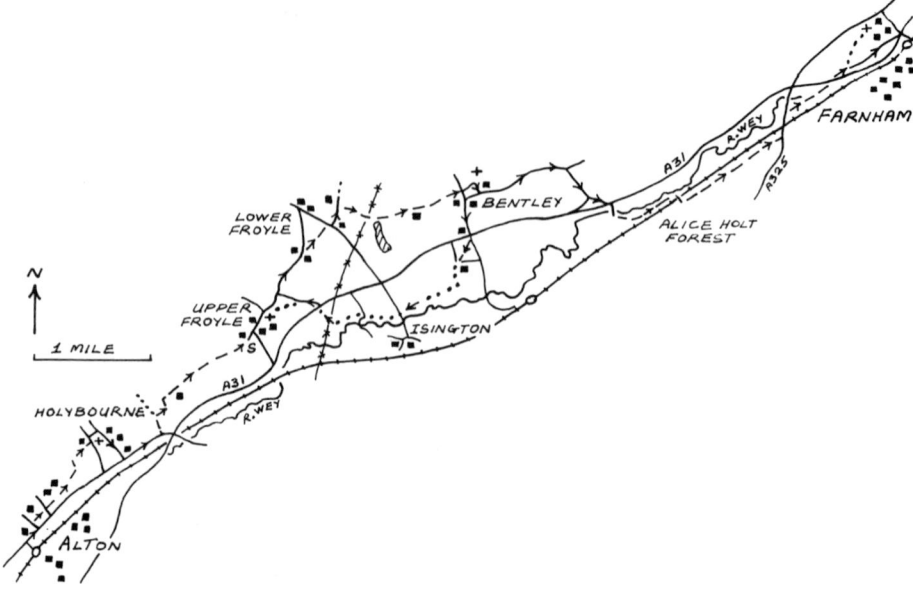

Turn left in the path here to follow the edge of the school field, and right after 100 yards or so into a path now along the 'top' edge of the field. The wire perimeter fence gives way to a timber one and this escorts you to a road at Holybourne. Turning left in the road and very soon right by Howards Farm Cottage, you will soon be at Holybourne church in its beautiful setting shared with old cottages and a pond. The pond is the source of the Holybourne stream which flows into the river Wey.

Having turned right at the church follow the pleasant lane down to the old London Road at Holybourne. Turn left in this and, after passing an interesting smithy building, look for a bridleway sign on the left opposite Vindomis Close. This is a departure from the Pilgrims' Way which is now the noisy A31, and takes you along a parallel route through Froyle and Bentley. A Department of the Environment notice at this point refers to the site of a small Roman town, probably Vindomis.

Go along the bridleway for 150 yards (that's about 200 man-size paces!) to the first gap in the hedge on the right. There is another

D of E notice here. From this gap go anti-clockwise around the field to another gap in the furthest corner, leading into Bonham's fruit and veg farm. If this is more difficult than it sounds (due to inconsiderate farming) it may be easier to make your exit from the bridleway later – through the second gap in the hedge after a further 100 yards – and approach Bonham's farm by a more direct line.

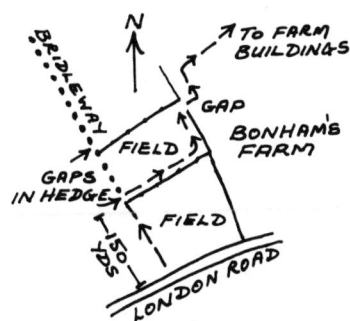

Once in the farm (fruit and veg directly ahead) turn left and follow the left-hand hedge for 50 yards (70 paces); then turn right to cross the farm in the direction of farm buildings. Pass to the left of the buildings along a curving farm track, then up to a stile beyond the last barn. A level stretch across a paddock links this stile with another at the far end of the hedge.

Now courage is the order of the day: you must trudge straight on across what may be a well and truly ploughed field. It's not quite as bad as it sounds: the furrows soon give way to a grassy field margin a few yards to the right of an electricity pylon (wires cross your route and Upper Froyle is directly ahead). This in its turn takes you downhill to join a track beside a large pond. The pleasant sight of wildfowl on the pond will help annul the trauma of that ploughed field!

The track will take you uphill to a grassy triangle at Upper Froyle. Go forward in the road ahead, ignoring a turning on the left, and follow it through (5) passing the church on your right, to a road junction. Go straight on from the junction to the last house on the left, Whiteway Cottage. Leave the road after a few yards through a gap on the right. A path soon runs under roadside beech trees (there is a war memorial on the opposite bank) and finally rejoins the road before a house called Butt Piece.

Leave the road immediately beyond the house, where a path will direct you down to a stile in the furthest corner of a field. After bypassing White House by way of a field-edge, a drive takes you down to the road at Lower Froyle. Turn right here (left for a shop and a pub) and first left into Hussey's Lane beside a pond overlooked by a pretty huddle of cottages.

Follow the lane to a path leaving from the right opposite Hussey's Farm (notice the fine Georgian front and the set of four oast houses). Make your way across a pasture to a stile about half way along its left-hand hedge, then stay with the hedge, but on the other side. Follow the hedge and a ditch to a stile in the field's far right-hand corner. Turn right from the stile and left after 40 yards where the fields intersect. This will take you under electricity wires and alongside a lake (take my word for it!) hidden by trees. Soon after this go forward (95 degrees) across a field to a point half way along a 'line' of trees. Hussey's Farm should be directly behind you.

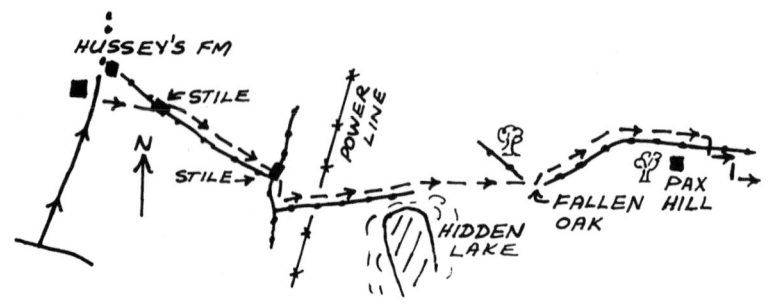

Now it's left and all fours under a massive fallen oak to make it to the next field! After that resume your previous direction (and up-right!) along the right-hand side of the field to a gap in the hedge just beyond Pax Hill School. Forward again, soon turning right at a field corner in a vegetable farm. Then go left after 100 yards to join another fieldside and a hopgarden before meeting the road at Jenkyn Place, Bentley.

Turn right in the road and left immediately for the church. Then right at the church by Well Cottage, and soon down to a T-junction. For the circular walk turn right at the T-junction and continue from page 31.

For the through route to Farnham go left to another road junction by Broadhatch Cottage. Then continue straight on for ¾ mile to the extremity of a wood on the right. Turn right at the road junction here (signposted to Farnham) and follow to a T-junction. The crossing is part of the original A31 (and the Pilgrims' Way) and there is an old signpost to prove it.

Turn left and go down to the new A31. Cross to Gravel Hill Road opposite and joing a good path on the left just beyond the river. Now there is ¾ mile of riverside path – part in the open, partly under trees – before going under a railway arch on the right where a path also comes in from the A31. Go through a kissing-gate on the left soon after leaving the arch and follow the railway to a stile and under trees. Now you are crossing from Hampshire into Surrey – congratulations!

After emerging from the trees a huge sand quarry rears its head on the right. At the far end of the quarry you will be ushered right, then left to join a hedge-lined track. When this turns right go forward across a cricket green (or around it, depending on the state of play!) to a road on the opposite side. Turn left and follow the road down and around, through a housing estate to the A325.

Left here and under the railway to a rough lane on the right, just before houses and an antique shop. The lane evolves into a pleasant riverside path prior to the A31. Cross the A31 diagonally to a path on the far side (look for a signpost under trees), following the river again and placing the A31 on your right.

Where the path becomes a gravel track it is possible to turn off left over the river along a path heading directly to Farnham town centre. For the railway station continue straight on past Farnham Maltings, over the A281 by the William Cobbett public house (where he was born in 1763), and forward along Abbey Street to traffic lights on the A31. Turn right there for the station.

Returning to Upper Froyle from Bentley: Having left Bentley church and turned right at the T-junction, follow the road to the next junction and turn left. This will take you down to the A31 by Bentley Community Centre, where there is an interesting covered panel giving a potted history of the area.

Cross the A31 to the road opposite and go along this for 60 yards to a stile on the right. Walking across the field half right with respect to the road (220 degrees) will take you to another stile in a hedge. You should make your way left across the next field to a stile in a wire fence at the centre of a group of houses.

Go right in a metalled drive here and follow it as it describes an anti-clockwise semicircle around a pond, overlooked by Green Farm. Turn left when this meets a lane (coming in from the A31) and fork right very soon into a track between hedges. (The left branch goes to a large farmhouse). The track follows the gardens of the house and ends at a farm gate in a field corner. Turn right immediately after the gate and walk this level route parallel to the river Wey, which is downhill on the left.

Go over two stiles in succession in the far right-hand corner of the pasture and, when in sight of a tennis court and a house ahead (Vine House), go over a stile on the right by an iron gate. Continue forward and cross a stream 20 yards to the right of the tennis court. This path has been diverted to its present alignment to avoid passing the front of the house but your OS Map may still show the original route.

Go straight on from the stream (and don't be dissuaded by the lack of an appropriate finger on the signpost!) uphill to a stile in the fence on the left after 200 yards. Descend a field to a stile on the drive serving Vine House, and turn right. That is the diversion over.

The drive terminates at a lane by Isington Mill. Spend a few moments of your time here to contemplate this fine building by the clear waters of the Wey. It was the home of Viscount Montgomery of Alamein until his death in 1970.

Now back to the crossing of the lane and along a hedge-lined path to a gate. From the gate your next objective is a hedgerow-corner on higher ground directly in line with a distant pylon, and the easiest approach to this is along the left-hand field-edge parallel to the river. Having reached the higher ground, go forward, with trees and a sloping field on the left, to a road. Turn right here and left immediately after the barns. It is a tight semi-circle around the barns and through nettles to a stile and a wide path overlooking the river. Another diversion over!

A stile at the end of this terraced path (before the second iron gate and overhead power lines) will place you in a sloping field on the right. Since the ploughman has obliterated the path here you will now find your compass invaluable! A 210 degree bearing will take you in a straight line across a large field to a gate beside the A31 – no trouble! Failing that, aim for the turning-point of a wire fence and go straight on uphill across the field, passing 100 yards to the left of a pylon.

Cross the A31 to a minor road opposite and follow this down to a drive on the left under an avenue of tall lime trees. Don't be perturbed by the 'Private' notice (this is a right-of-way) but go along the drive towards the church and school. Stop 120 yards short of the church, cross a stile on the right and make for the road at Upper Froyle.

Historical Notes

Alton: At its heart, Alton is still a homely, pleasant town. If time is short I suggest a quick circuit starting from the Curtis Museum in High Street: firstly along Church Street; then across St Lawrence churchyard to Amery Hill and Amery Street and into the attractive little Market Square, with its beautifully renovated Town Hall. Then along Market Street and back into High Street.

In Church Street opposite the Allen Gallery you will see Geale's Almshouses, built by one of Cromwell's officers, Captain Thomas Geale, for eight poor people. Impressions left by musket balls on the walls and inner door of St Lawrence's church bear witness to an affray which took place in 1643 during the Civil War, when Colonel Boles and his men made a valiant but unsuccessful stand against invading Parliamentary forces. The oldest object in the church is the Saxon font in its interesting position mounted on a millstone. The font was thrown out in Victorian times and rediscovered years later in a Churchwarden's garden!

'Sweet Fanny Adams' is very much part of the spoken English language, but Sweet Fanny actually lived and died here in Alton! Victim of a savage murder Fanny is buried in the town cemetery north of Church Street. On the brighter side, Alton possesses its own little nature reserve, King's Pond. This lies off Paper Mill Lane south-west of the railway station, and is home to many species of wild flowers, birds and waterfowl. The reserve is easily accessible to the public.

Vindomis: Discovered in 1969 during the building of Alton's bypass, the small Roman town had an estimated population of 2,500 people and was situated at the crossing of two Roman roads, Silchester to Chichester and Winchester to London. Excavation work took place on both sides of London Road from 1969 onwards.

Upper Froyle: The Lord Mayor Treloar College for physically hand-icapped children takes up much of the village space, including the Georgian manor house and clunch-built (chalk stone) Froyle Place.

33

Lord Mayor Treloar's compassionate concern for the plight of London's crippled children led to the foundation of the college (originally in Alton) in 1908. The Lower School is here at Froyle, while the Upper School is at Holybourne. My impression is that it is a very caring, happy community.

As you walk through the village you may be intrigued by the small statues standing in niches on the fronts of the houses. These were brought over from Italy by Sir Hubert Miller, one-time Lord of the Manor, who died in 1941.

Farnham to Puttenham

Introduction: With the A31 keeping its hold on the Pilgrims' Way for a further two miles, we follow instead the enjoyable route of the North Downs Way as far as Binton Cottage. After meeting the Pilgrims' Way at Sandy Cross there soon follows a most satisfying road walk to Puttenham – through the lovely village of Seale and beneath the impressive slopes of the Hog's Back.

The circular walk from Seale makes full use of the North Downs Way when returning from Puttenham, including the invigorating high ground of Puttenham Common.

Circular Walk: Seale – Puttenham – Puttenham Common – Seale
The walk is 4 miles (6.5 km) and starts at **(6)** on page 37 in Seale village. There is parking possible opposite the community centre in School Hill in the village.

Pilgrims' Route: Farnham to Puttenham
The walk is 6½ miles (10.5 km) and begins at Farnham Station. There is a convenient car park off Downing Street.

To return to Farnham by public transport buses run hourly (214/215) and 2 hourly on Sunday (453). Bus stop is on the A31.

The Walk: From the railway station go downhill and turn right at the A31 crossing. Leave the A31 for a lane on the right after 100 yards and follow this for about the same distance to a T-junction just before a red-brick house. Turn right here and left immediately to join a rough track parallel to the A31 and, later, the river. On arrival at The Kiln go right into a path and under the railway.

The path runs alongside meadows to a T-junction under trees. Turn left here and go along to a stile on the right after 50 yards (ie not straight on!). Beyond the stile a lovely open area of grass and trees, and 'Culverlands' beautifully situated on the right. Two more stiles

35

and you are out onto a quiet road. Turn left into this road and soon left again into Moor Park Lane. (Had you gone straight on for one mile you would have come near to the ruins of Waverley Abbey, the first Cistercian monastery in England, founded in 1128.

Go along Moor Park Lane, over the river Wey and past the entrance to Moor Park House, once the home of Sir William Temple. This is where William Temple's secretary, Jonathan Swift, wrote the well-known *Tale of a Tub*, published in 1704. Go uphill in Compton Way and, when this curves right, keep straight on over a stile and soon into fields beside a wire fence. You will pass two cattle troughs and enter a wood at its near left-hand corner. From this point you should see Farnham Castle 2 miles westward (285 degrees).

Straight on now through the wood until you are led down a few steps from a stile to a crossing path. Turn right in this and follow a bank and ditch for 100 yards under beech trees to a footpath junction. Turning left here (North Downs Way) you will notice that a diminished ramp and ditch remains on the left. Houses and a private drive appear on the right and you are soon at a road.

Turn left in the road and, after 20 yards, right into a path between fences; then soon to another road. A right turn here will take you to Farnham Golf Club. (If in desperate need of a shop or a pub, stay in this road to The Sands!) Otherwise turn left in Blighton Lane just beyond the Golf Club House.

When the road starts to curve left ¼ mile from the club house you will see the North Downs Way leaving from the right, opposite a wide

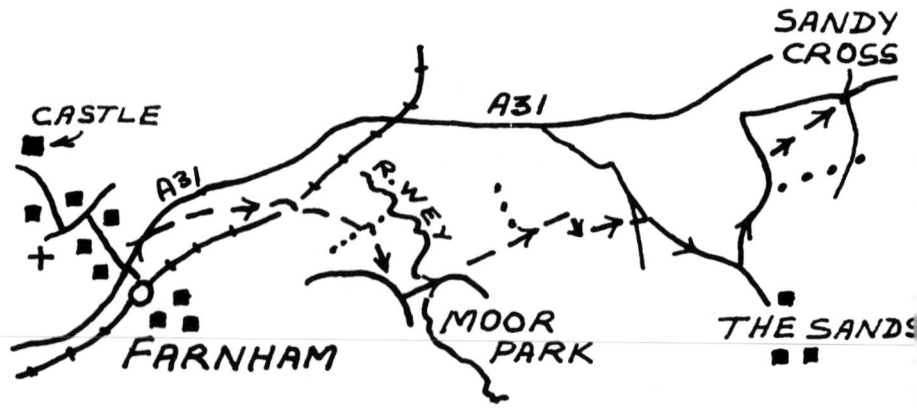

verge. Don't go that way but stay in the road as far as the wrought iron entrance gates of Pightle House on the right. Immediately after the gates turn right into a fenced path under trees. Now keep absolutely straight on until you come to a crossroad (Sandy Cross). The Pilgrims' Way at last – and a seat for weary Pilgrims!

Going forward from the crossing you will pass Seale Plant Market on the left; and where the pavement terminates, a tarmac path (behind the hedge on the left) will take you safely into Seale.

(6) Go straight on through the village to the war memorial – passing the church on the left; then turn left into Puttenham Road. You now have a beautiful 2 mile stretch of quiet road (still the Pilgrims' Way) to Puttenham. You will pass well cared for 16th century Eastend Farm just outside Seale, and Shoelands (circa 1616) at the half-way point. And soon coming into view is the last remaining hop garden in Surrey.

On arrival at Puttenham's Post Office (not 'The Old Post Office') turn right into Lascombe Lane if you are on the circular walk, and continue from below. Otherwise, keep straight on through the village to the church. (Do take a look at the village in any case!)

Returning to Seale from Puttenham: For this return trip we make use of the North Downs Way for all but the last few hundred yards.

From Puttenham's Post Office go along Lascombe Lane and keep straight on when this divides at a fork. You will pass a cottage called Clouds Hill at the summit of the lane, after which the lane evolves

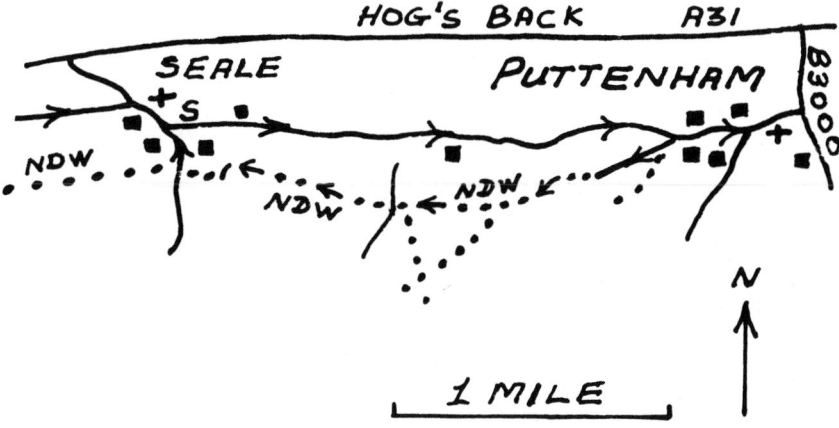

into a sunken path. You are soon out into the open, with a fine view along the valley – including Seale church.

At a Y-junction ahead take the right-hand branch along a wide grassy path (270 degrees), with trees on the right and open heathland left, and follow the acorn signs to the bottom of the hill. Ignore a bridleway going left here, then soon turn left into a tarmac drive in front of an unnamed cottage. Proceed a few steps along this 'private drive' and turn right into a path under trees. Follow this up to a stile ahead, ignoring the stile leading into a field on the left.

Next go between a thick line of trees on the left, and a new planting on the right – with a view of the Hog's Back beyond. The path passes through an outcrop of trees, follows the edge of a mature coniferous wood (mature enough for felling) and turns left over a stile at the end of the wood. With a pasture on the right, follow the path as it enters the wood, then soon turn right at a T-junction. The left-hand branch is private. Keep right at the fork ahead and continue forward to a road. Turn right here and follow the road down into Seale.

Historical Notes

The accepted route of the Pilgrims' Way between Farnham and Guildford is through the villages of Seale and Puttenham. The Hog's Back ridge may have been used as an alternative. This runs parallel at a higher level, avoiding what would have been low-lying woodland in earlier days, but paying the price in terms of exposure to the elements. Since this ridge now carries the A31 there is no question of us using it today, even with the fine views on offer!

Farnham: Certainly one of the finest towns in Southern England, perhaps in all England. Much photographed Castle Street presents a magnificent aspect of red-brick Georgian frontages, with Farnham Castle rounding off the scene at the far end. It is worthwhile walking to the top of the street and ascending the tree-shaded 'Blind Bishop's Steps' (seven flights of seven steps with seven paces between them), for this will give you a close view of the castle keep. Pay an entrance fee to enjoy the view from the top of the keep, and another for the castle proper with its 'Great Hall and other rooms' (the latter open on Wednesday afternoons only).

Making your way back down Castle Street notice the homely terrace of almshouses dated 1619 and, turning right into The

Borough, follow this through to West Street. Here you will find the much acclaimed three-storey Willmer House and Sandford House, and many impressive Georgian doorways. Willmer House is home to Farnham's excellent little Town Museum.

Among the special delights of Farnham are the little side streets and alleyways, where it is a pleasure to walk. In a different class is the popular Lion and Lamb Yard (previously a brewery yard) with modern shops in an attractively restored setting. Also restored for modern use as an arts and community centre are the extensive 19th century buildings of Farnham Maltings. These lie beside the river Wey and on the final leg of the walk from Alton. A little east of the Maltings (in Bridge Square) you will find the public house where William Cobbett was born in 1763. Previously The Jolly Farmer, it is now named after him. This countryman of many parts – reformer, author, politician, farmer – lies buried in St Andrew's churchyard. He is perhaps best known for his book *Rural Rides*.

Seale is a delightful village a little above the valley floor, well away from the Hog's Back and, depending on how the wind blows, from the noise of traffic. Walls, barns and church raised in 'clunch' – stone cut from the local chalk levels. First to catch your eye as you approach from the Pilgrims' Way is Manor Farm Craft Centre with its fascinating display of wood, glass and jewellery fashioned by dedicated craftsmen and women in a group of converted stables. And there's a restaurant and tea room to add to the pleasure!

The church of St Lawrence lost its carved screen and its musicians' gallery during extensive 'restoration' work in 1860 – 'destruction work' might be a more apt description! Retained are its Norman timbers in porch and vestry doorways, its ancient piscina and its 12th century font, while the tower still echoes to the sound of a 16th century tenor bell – in a tuneful peal of six.

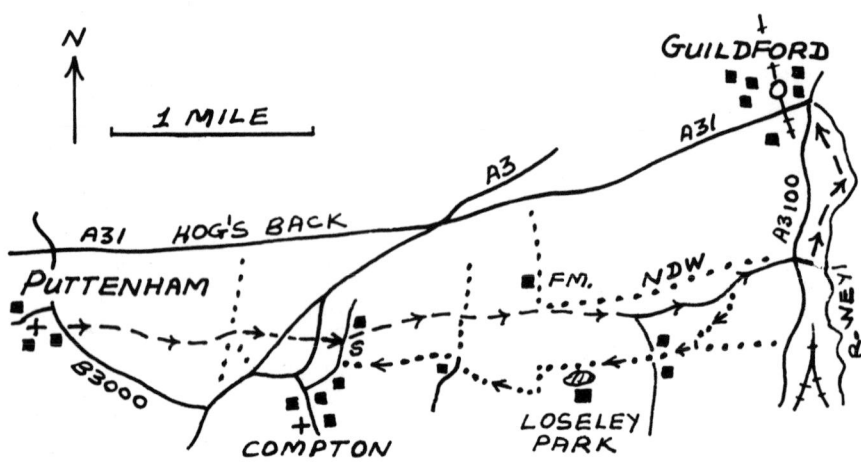

N

1 MILE

A3

A31   HOG'S BACK

A31

GUILDFORD

A3100

PUTTENHAM

R. WEY!

B3000

FM.   NDW

COMPTON

S

LOSELEY
PARK

WALK FIVE

Puttenham to Guildford

Introduction: An easy-going walk that starts by following the edge of Puttenham Heath and ends at the pleasant waters of the river Wey, allowing time to contemplate the attractive old houses at Puttenham and Compton – the latter requiring a short diversion from the through route.

The circular walk passes close to Loseley House, a fine Elizabethan mansion open to the public and known to many for its dairy products – and its friendliness!

Circular Walk: Compton – Mount Brown – Loseley Park – Compton
The walk is 4 miles (6.5 km) and starts from (**7**) on page 42 at the Watts Gallery, Compton, where the curator has kindly given permission to park. There is also parking space by the Watts Cemetery.

Pilgrims' Route: Puttenham to Guildford
The walk is 5 miles (8 km) and begins at Puttenham Church. Parking is available in the layby on the B3000 near its junction with The Street.

To return to Puttenham by public transport buses run hourly Mon–Sat (214/215) and 2 hourly on Sunday (453).

The Walk: With Puttenham church on your right, go along The Street to the busy B3000 road (The Heath). Turn right in this and left after 100 yards into a rough track signposted 'North Downs Way' (not the golf club drive). This will place the Harvester Restaurant behind you. You will soon pass Pilgrims' Way Cottage and the golf and cricket clubs on the right.

One redeeming feature of this over-used part of the Way is a small cottage with a well cared for front garden. After passing the entrance to Greyfriars Farm the Way improves and it is all very pleasant again.

Beyond a scattering of houses a branch goes off to the right. Ignore

41

this and continue straight on along the Public Bridleway. You will pass Questors, a large house on the left before negotiating a slight twist in the path. Continuing straight on at a crossing beyond that twist, you will eventually pass under the improved A3 road. Beyond this, the old A3 road-bridge is topped by two prominent wooden crosses, put there to remind motorists that they are crossing the Pilgrims' Way. The old bridge was designed by the distinguished architect Sir Edwin Lutyens.

Having passed beneath these bridges you will shortly arrive at a quieter road. Turn left here (right for Compton) and go forward the short distance to Watt's Gallery (7). Branch half-right along a sandy track (a bucket and spade would seem in order!) passing to the right of the gallery.

In about ½ mile you will approach a collection of barns of one sort or another before going uphill under trees and over a crossing track. After another ½ mile ignore a track that runs downhill from a gap on the left to Conduit Farm, watching for the view of Loseley Park on the right. It is here that we take leave of the North Downs Way which passes through the gap and turns right to follow the upper edge of a field. We – like all good pilgrims – continue straight on!

You will eventually meet a road at a sharp hairpin bend. Take the upper arm of this (Sandy Lane) and follow it past some desirable suburban houses. Just before the road drops steeply downhill, another road, signposted to Mount Brown Police Headquarters, leaves from the right. Those returning to Compton on the circular walk should take that road (The Drive) and continue below.

The through route is steeply downhill in Sandy Lane to the main road (A3100). Turn right here then first left into Ferry Lane. (For St Catherine's Chapel, and an excellent view, climb the grassy bank on the right). Ignore the track going off to the right and follow Ferry Lane to a railway bridge and down to the river Wey. If you are staying in the Pilgrims' Way turn right along the river bank to the footbridge, and continue from (8) on page 48. To end the walk at Guildford turn left and follow the river bank the ½ mile or so into town.

Returning to Compton from Mount Brown: Having turned right from the Pilgrims' Way into The Drive, go along this for a short distance to a path on the right. The path passes between houses and garages before skirting the grounds of the Police Headquarters. It eventually turns left around a sports field and meets a T-junction with another path after 100 yards.

Turn right at the T-junction and follow the path (later a road) to the crossing at Littleton. Join the short track opposite and go along this to a stile, passing a Youth Centre on the left. Go over the stile and straight on across a field to another stile and gate at the far end.

Now hold it there! The path appears to go left from this point along a well-trodden route. However, the right-of-way is not down there but straight on across two fields to a stile on the far side (260 degrees). All is not lost if you do take the left-hand turn (as I did); simply circumnavigate the said fields by taking two consecutive right-hand turns.

Assuming you are in the correct orientation that last stile will lead you forward along the right-hand side of a large pond, a haunt of Canada geese. And now the centrepiece of this return route to Compton: Loseley Park, in view on your left. Soon after this you will be confronted by a crossing track and two pairs of iron gates. These are easily bypassed by virtue of two convenient stiles, enabling you to continue in the forward direction, but in another field.

After 30 yards the path turns left, with the field still on the right and a hedgerow of sorts on the left. Leave the field after 50 yards by going over a stile on the left and resuming the same direction, heading towards a T-junction at the entrance to Loseley Park. Do visit the Park if you have time; you will find it a most pleasant and interesting experience.

Turn right at the T-junction into a long, straight drive lined with chestnut trees. A third of a mile of this and you are met by another junction at Palsted Manor. The Manor itself is approached by a left turn along a lane, but you should turn right into a narrow, sunken bridleway, for 35 yards only – to a path on the left.

Haul yourself up the steps here and into the light of day, where there is a garden left and a field right, and another sighting of the Hog's Back. The path soon runs between wire fences and eventually to a stile, then straight on again, having crossed a ditch. With the ditch now on the right the path continues to a T-junction with another path at the far right-hand corner of a field. A few steps right and then left along a concrete farm drive, heading towards the barns at Coneycroft Farm.

For the Watts Gallery take the path to the right of the farm buildings. For the Watts cemetery and Compton go left around the farm to a road, and turn left there.

Historical Notes

Puttenham: Apart from an inverted U-shaped curve at Puttenham the Pilgrims' Way describes a relatively straight line west to east as far as the river Wey south of Guildford. Hilaire Belloc in his book *The Old Road* contended that the curve at Puttenham was a later development and that the Way originally passed south of the church on ground now occupied by The Priory. Whether he was aware that a 19th century occupant of the Priory re-routed the road because it passed in front of his windows, I'm not sure!

The church of St John the Baptist looks westward over Puttenham's 'Street', a street of handsome red brick cottages. Puttenham Priory of 1762 is best seen from the south side of the churchyard. While you are in the churchyard you cannot fail to see the Old Well, rediscovered in 1972 when a yew tree suddenly disappeared into the ground! A short distance from the church the oast houses and barns of Gray's Home Farm now form part of residential development.

Compton: A medley of old and new houses strung out along the busy B3000 just south of the Pilgrims' Way. The ancient church of St Nicholas, parts of which date back to Saxon times, is tucked away behind the wall of Eastbury manor. It possesses a beautiful and unique upper sanctuary where 'sacred' relics may have been placed on display. The sanctuary is fronted by a balustrade which is one of the earliest pieces of Norman woodwork in the country.

Situated right on the Pilgrims' Way is the Watts Gallery, where paintings and sculpture by the prolific Victorian artist George Frederick Watts may be viewed. The Watts cemetery lies, as does Watts himself, between the gallery and the village. Here you may (or may not!) be attracted by an ornate chapel set up in his memory by his widow.

Loseley Park: Not everyone would associate the Loseley brand-name with the finest Elizabethan mansion in Surrey. As well as being a magnificent house in its own right containing many important works of art, Loseley is noted for its pedigree Jersey cattle and for the dairy products which carry the Loseley name. The House is open to the public from June to September, Wednesday to Saturday 2–5 pm. Tractor rides around the farm include an opportunity to see Loseley's numerous breeds of sheep, pigs and poultry.

St Catherine's Chapel stands on a hill overlooking the river Wey and dates back to the 14th century. The hill may have been an important staging-post for pilgrims contemplating the river crossing. Its height alone would provide a useful view of the state of the river and the marshy ground beyond.

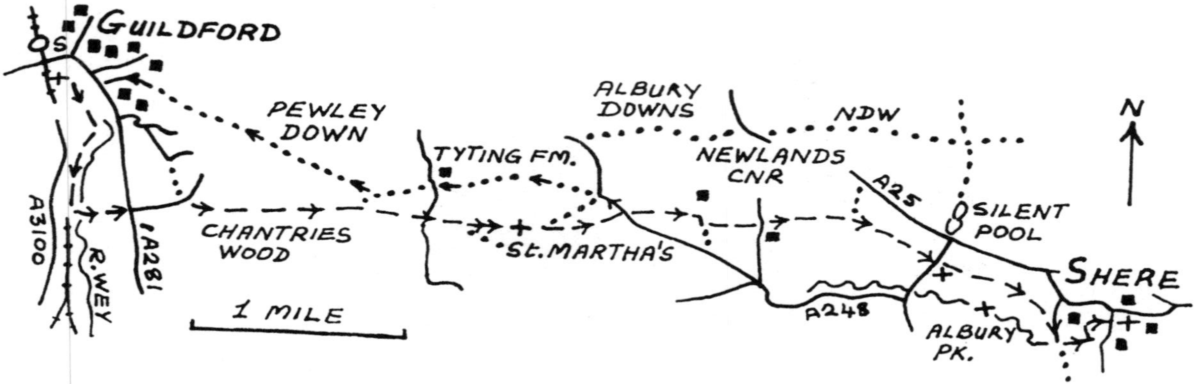
GUILDFORD
S
PEWLEY DOWN
ALBURY DOWNS
NDW
N
TYTING FM.
NEWLANDS CNR
A25
SILENT POOL
A3100
R.WEY
A281
CHANTRIES WOOD
St.MARTHA'S
SHERE
A248
ALBURY PK.
1 MILE

Guildford to Shere

Introduction: The day starts with an easy stroll along the towpath of the river Wey and meets the Pilgrims' Way at a footbridge below St Catherine's Hill. The Way soon runs inside Chantries Wood, but not so deeply that it obscures the fine view across fields to Pewley Down. It makes the steep ascent of St Martha's Hill to St Martha's church, where the reward is a breathtaking view of the Tillingbourne valley to the south. After descending the hill we follow pleasant paths and bridleways leading to the picturesque village of Shere.

For the circular walk we double back from below St Martha's Hill and return to Guildford through Tyting Farm and over Pewley Hill.

Circular Walk: Guildford – St Martha's – Pewley Down – Guildford
The walk is 6½ miles (10.5 km) and begins at Guildford Station. There are numerous car parks in the town.

Pilgrims' Route: Guildford to Shere
The walk is 6 miles (9.7 km) and also begins at Guildford Station, with numerous car parks available in the town.

To return to Guildford by public transport buses run 2 hourly Mon–Sat only (22). There is also an infrequent rail service from Gomshall station, one mile east of Shere.

The Walk: From Guildford's railway station cross over at the traffic lights, pass to the right of the new Wey House, and go along Park Street. Turn left into High Street by St Nicholas' church and walk towards a pedestrianised river bridge, without actually crossing it. You now have a view of the uphill portion of High Street with the overhanging Guildhall Clock. Before turning right into Millmead, spare a few moments to read the inscriptions on the old bridge, detailing its construction and reconstruction.

Along Millmead a sculpture on a riverside lawn depicting Alice in

Wonderland is a reminder of Lewis Carroll's long association with Guildford. Cross the river by a footbridge at the end of Millmead and turn right to follow the canal bank. Make your way to the end of the park where canal and river meet; then turn right and follow the river bank for ½ mile to a footbridge.

(8) This is where Hilaire Belloc and his companion 'borrowed' a boat and crossed the river using a walking stick as an oar. They placed money in the boat and pleaded their 'grave necessity' as the owner of the boat 'protested with great violence'!

Cross the footbridge and follow the clear path alongside a marshy area. The path soon turns right and leads you straight on across a meadow and a sportsfield. A gap will place you on a road and into clearly-marked Pilgrims' Way (a fully-fledged road) directly opposite. Looking back you will see the chapel ruin on St Catherine's Hill. A magnificent row of lime trees escorts you along Pilgrims' Way. When this road curves slightly left beyond the limes you should launch into the metalled drive on the right labelled 'North Downs Way'.

The track meets Chantries Cottage before running beside Chantries Wood. When after ½ mile it passes the entrance to South Warren Farm keep straight on at a junction (ie not through the gate leading into the wood). Stay with the track as it bobs in and out of the shade, finally to meet a road. North Downs Way acorns will keep you on course.

Turn left in the road and soon join a path on the right by Southernway cottage. A speed limit sign marks the spot. The path takes you up past a small car park and out onto a very pleasant piece of heathland – a good place to gather strength for the ascent of St Martha's Hill. But hold on to your sandwiches – there's a seat with a view half-way up the hill, and more at the top!

Following the timber fence on the right enter the wood and go steeply uphill to St Martha's church, ignoring a branch on the right where the path steepens. If you enter the church you will have the good fortune to be conducted through its history by a very able guide.

Make your way to the gate at the far side (east) of the churchyard. Here you will find a memorial to Yvonne Arnaud, the actress and musician who died in 1958. Go downhill from that gate, maintaining your previous eastward direction, with the Tillingbourne Valley down on your right.

At a Y-junction lower down, the Pilgrims' Way takes leave of the North Downs Way. So ignore the acorn waymark beckoning you off to the left at this point and continue straight on. Very soon after this, on your right, you will find a signpost for the Downs Link. This is a long distance path linking the North and South Downs. Ignore this also, and continue straight on, passing a Second World War pill box on the left. The pill box is about 50 yards from the previous Y-junction.

The next item for your attention is a Surrey County Council notice board complete with map of the area, and a three-way fork in the path. Take the middle branch, which leads down to a secluded parking area beside a road. There is a notice board here also, giving details of services and opening times at St Martha's church. For the circular walk turn left in the road and continue from page 50.

To continue the walk to Shere turn right and then left into a fenced bridleway after 40 yards. If it is a weekend you will doubtless see cars and people at the ever popular Newlands Corner up on the downs.

The bridleway meets a T-junction after ⅓ mile, the left arm going to a farm. Turn right here, and left beside an iron gate after 50 yards. In addition to the waymark arrows, a Friend of Pilgrims has kindly splashed orange paint on the posts and stiles to help us on our way. The path goes uphill to join the left edge of a wood, then through a gate into a path under trees, and down to a lane.

Cross the lane to a rough track under trees opposite. There are two houses on the right where the hedge-lined track makes its way across fields, and a cottage at the end of the next ⅓ mile. Now don't repeat my error of turning left here (and being almost laid low by thistles and broad beans!) but continue straight on, with the cottage immediately to your right. There's an iron gate and stile very soon, leading into a track. After 80 yards you will arrive at a junction of ways with a timber yard in view ahead.

Your direction is straight on along a waymarked path, not the wide track running down to the timber yard. The path takes you to the right of a large metal barn and on to the entrance drive to Albury Sand Pit. Beware of lorries! Cross the drive to a path opposite and proceed along the left edge of a wood, with a field on the left and the A25 beyond that. A sequence of stiles and fields then leads to a road, almost opposite a commanding piece of Victorian Gothic, the Irving-ite church (see Historical Notes).

For a short but pleasant diversion to the Silent Pool (see Historical Notes) turn left in the road, then left in the A25 and soon right just before a car park; otherwise cross the road to a track opposite, beside a post-box. The Irvingite church will then be on your right. A stile at the end of that short track leads you into a field. An ornate chimney-pot will be the first solid piece of Albury Park Estate to come into view. Keep well to the left of this – and the cottage to which it is anchored – as you make your way across the field to a stile and gate.

The stile will place you in Silver Wood, from which you will later emerge via an iron kissing-gate. While you are crossing the next field to its far right-hand corner you will see more pieces of the Albury estate. From that field corner you will pass under trees to meet a lane. Turn right in the lane and follow this down to a footbridge over the Tillingbourne stream. Go left immediately beyond the footbridge and then accompany the stream to a gate that leads on to a rough drive. Turn left into the drive (still following the stream), finally entering Shere beside the ford in Rectory Lane.

Returning to Guildford from St Martha's Hill: From the parking area below St Martha's Hill turn left in the road (Guildford Road). When this soon turns right go straight on beside Keeper's Cottage, ignoring the North Downs Way as it crosses here. A gate soon leads you forward along a level path, with a field left and a wood right. The path evolves into a track and passes through Tyting Farm to a lane. This is Halfpenny Lane. Also in the vicinity are Halfpenny Copse and Farthing Copse, Great Halfpenny Farm and Little Halfpenny Farm! These all remind us of the toll roads of earlier days.

Cross the lane to what soon becomes a very sandy track. When you have hauled yourself through this, almost as far as the wood ahead, turn half-right into a long, straight hedge-lined path. As you now head up towards Pewley Down you should see the suburbs of Guildford; also (to the south of Guildford) the ruined chapel on St Catherine's Hill. At a three-way fork under trees at the end of this long path, take the central branch, which is straight on, following a thick hedge on your left; eventually up to a topograph and viewpoint near the summit of the hill.

With your OS map at the ready you may be able to indentify a place or two in this impressive panorama. It is gratifying to read on the topograph that Pewley Down was given to the public by the Friary Brewery in 1920, and that the hill is 113.339 metres above sea level. That's 0.001% accuracy!

A path from the top of the hill will take you towards the upper of two large houses, where a road terminates. This road is Pewley Hill which takes you right down into Guildford, and provides a good view of the Cathedral and the University.

Historical Notes

There can be little doubt that pilgrims en route to Canterbury were ferried across the river Wey more or less where the footbridge stands today, since this is directly in line with the Pilgrims' Way east and west of the river. At this point the river is overlooked by a 14th century chapel (now a ruin) on St Catherine's Hill, and its siting here may well have been important to the physical and spiritual needs of pilgrims passing this way. Primitive travellers probably crossed the river at Shalford ('Shallow Ford') one mile upstream. Without the convenience of a ferry this diversion to a more fordable part of the river was unavoidable.

Although it is generally accepted that the Pilgrims' Way mounted the summit of St Martha's Hill and continued just north of both Weston Wood and Albury Park, other possible routes have been suggested: that it passed through Tyting Farm (the return route of our circular walk); that it followed the southern slope of Albury Downs; that it passed through the grounds of Albury Park.

Guildford: An ideal place to take a break in your exploration of the Pilgrims' Way. But I'll not promise a rest-day, for there is much to see!

The Castle was built in Henry II's time and is a prominent landmark in the town. Its Keep is open to the public and there are unparalleled views from the top. The Castle Gardens are a breath-taking sight from Spring through to Autumn. In High Street the Guildhall proudly displays its famous overhanging clock. Close by is Abbot's Hospital, an almshouse of 1619 and open to the public at limited times. In Quarry Street (near the Castle) the museum has items relating to the history and archaeology of Guildford and Surrey, and a collection of needlework dating back to the 17th century. The Chestnuts in Castle Hill is where Lewis Carroll died in 1898, but the house is not open to the public.

The old Town Mill beside the river Wey is now linked with the modern Yvonne Arnaud Theatre. The river is part of the National Trust's 'River Wey Nagivations'. This runs (or flows!) from Godalming in the south to the Thames at Weybridge, a distance of 20 miles.

St Mary's church in Quarry Street is Guildford's oldest building. The modern Guildford Cathedral is about ¾ mile from the town centre, near the University. Its foundation stone was laid in 1936, but the building was not consecrated until 1961.

St Martha's church: Although early in appearance the church dates back to 1848–50 when it was rebuilt from its previously derelict condition, a condition partly brought about by an explosion in nearby Chilworth gunpowder factory in 1745. Of special interest to us on our 'pilgrimage' is a piece of stone inscribed with crosses – apparently by pilgrims who passed this way in the Middle Ages. It has been suggested that a certain amount of confusion during the passage of time has resulted in 'St Martyr's' becoming 'St Martha's', giving a measure of validity to the tradition that several Christians were martyred here around the year AD 600. The church is open to view at certain times, and services are held every Sunday.

The Irvingite Church was built in 1840 by Henry Drummond of nearby Albury Park for the Catholic Apostolic Church, a sect founded by Edward Irving, the 'sensational preacher and prophet'. That Irving's activities, and those of his church, did not fall into line with current thinking is confirmed by his being condemned, deposed and excommunicated by various ecclesiastical institutions. Services are no longer held in the church and it is usually kept locked.

The Silent Pools (there are two of them) make a pleasant diversion from the walk. Judging by the wear and tear of the waterside paths, many other people share this sentiment!

A 19th century novelist depicted a beautiful maiden by the name of Emma, who, when swimming naked in one of these ponds, was surprised by the 'wicked' Prince John. In her embarrassment she waded deeper and deeper until, out of her depth, she let out a great cry, and drowned. Come here of a moonlit night and you will hear that cry echoing across the water!

Shere to Dorking

Introduction: A walk to gladden the eye and the feet: the delightful village of Shere; the bracing heathland of Abinger Roughs; the breathtaking views of the Downs; the lovely 'Denbies Coach Road' – a hillside track especially beautiful in the flower-laden days of summer.

The circular walk starts from Dorking and follows pleasant lowland paths to Westcott; then uphill (very steeply so in one place) to join the Pilgrims' Way back to Dorking.

Circular Walk: Dorking – Westcott – Coach Road – Dorking
The walk is 4 miles (6.4 km) and starts at **(9)** on page 56, in Station Road in Dorking. There is parking possible in Curtis Road or Glebe Road nearby.

Pilgrims' Route: Shere to Dorking
The walk is 6½ miles (10.5 km) and begins at Shere Church. There is roadside parking just south of the church.

To return to Shere by public transport, buses run 2 hourly Mon–Sat only (22). There is an infrequent rail service from Dorking West and Dorking Deepdene stations to Gomshall, one mile east of Shere.

The Walk: From St James' church at Shere go uphill in a narrow path running between a hedge and a fence. This path starts and ends at a gate, the second being at the top of the hill. Turn left after the second gate and join a path along the left-hand edge of a field. Stay in this good path until you meet a T-junction by three houses, including Gravel Pits Farmhouse. Turn left into the drive here and follow this round to a road.

Cross the road to Highview opposite, and go forward along this until it curves left at Goose Green. Before passing under the railway bridge along Tower Hill, notice the attractive Malthouse Cottages, with their curved braces and central 'hall-house'. Ignore the first drive on the left after the bridge (leading to a large house) and turn into the next after a few yards. This soon shapes into a path along the left side of farm buildings and passes a white farmhouse on the right. Turn right at a T-junction ahead into a farm track and bear left with it immediately by Twiga Lodge, resuming your forward direction.

At Southbrooks Farmhouse take the left branch of the Y-junction and join a path on the right directly after the house (ie don't stay in the drive). Following the left-hand edge of a field you will rejoin the drive later. This crosses a stream and soon meets the A25. Turn right in the A25 and first left into a lane at Abinger Hammer – just before the hammer; but wait for the turning of the hour, and you will see the smith strike!

At the summit of the lane go through a gate on the right, sign-posted 'National Trust Bridleway to Abinger Roughs'. Follow the right-hand edge of a field to a gate in the far right-hand corner. Cross the end of a sandy track and go forward into The Roughs as far as an open grassy area within the wood. At the junction of ways here (five of them) take the half-left branch (60 degrees) and follow this up through the woods and down to a stile. Continue forward just inside the wood, with a field on the left (you need not cross the stile).

Keeping close to the fields, you will pass a memorial cross on the right before encountering a road. The cross marks the spot where Bishop Samuel Wilberforce was killed after a fall from his horse in 1873. Samuel was a son of William Wilberforce MP, who dedicated his life to the abolition of the Slave Trade.

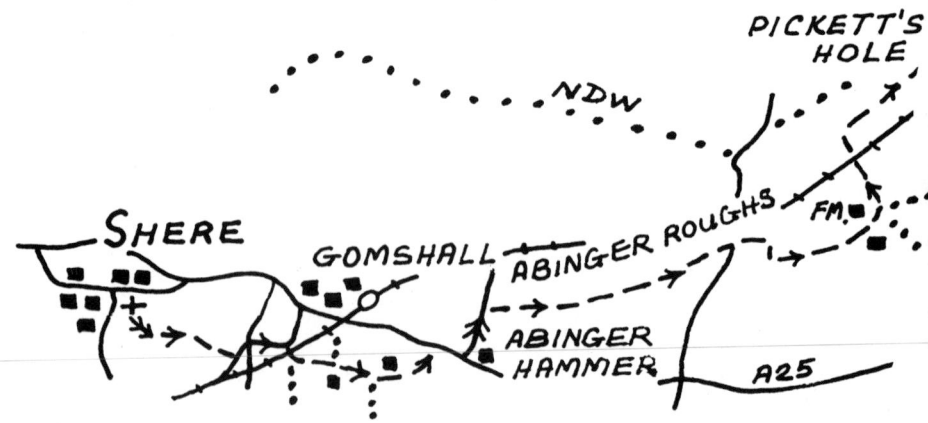

Cross the road to a bridleway opposite and follow this as it skirts the field edge, with Wotton Estate woodland on the right. In the distance the spire of Ranmore Common church ('Cubitt's Finger') will be in view half left. At a junction of ways just beyond Park Farm, take the left-hand branch, aiming directly for the downs. The track runs uphill and joins woodland at a gate, after which it turns right and divides at a Y-junction. Take the right-hand 'footpath only' branch and follow the long, level path under trees, just above the fields.

(There is an opportunity to enjoy a magnificent view by diverting uphill in a waymarked path at one point but don't forget to come back!). The path describes a left-hand semicircle at another point, before resuming its direct route. After one mile from the earlier Y-junction you will come out into the open at a crossing, adjacent to a Forestry Commission notice board. Continuing straight on from the crossing you will soon encounter another track making a hair-pin bend ahead. Go left and uphill in this to a stile and a gate.

You are now on the straight, gently climbing Coach Road, once used as an approach to Denbies, a 19th century house (now demolished) on Ranmore Common. In summer the chalk grassland

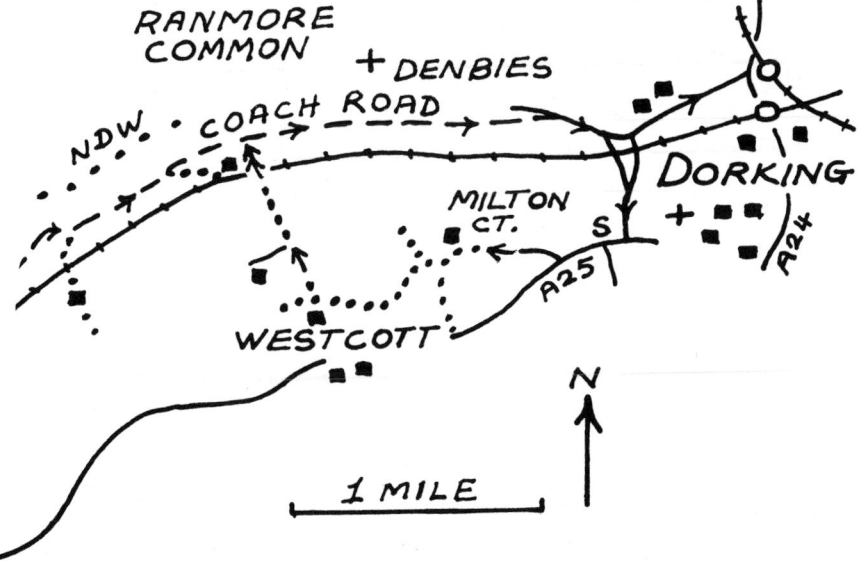

slopes are bright with a colourful array of wildflowers and their attendant butterflies.

(10) When after ¾ mile you reach the end of an overhanging canopy of yew, take the right-hand branch at a Y-junction. After a further mile go half right into a path under trees just before the west entrance gate to South Lodge. This will lead you to a tarmaced path running beside a school and down to Ranmore Road.

For Dorking main-line station (and the through route) or Dorking Deepdene station cross over and go along Ashcombe Road (that's ¾ mile; followed by a right turn in the A24 London Road for Dorking Deepdene).

For the town centre go right in Ranmore Road. This joins Station Road which in turn meets West Street (A25) at a T-junction. For the town centre, turn left.

Circular Walk from Dorking: (9) Having turned right out of Station Road go along West Street and Westcott Road (A25) for ¼ mile to the third turning on the right, Milton Court Lane. The lane soon becomes a sandy track and you will have, I trust, a good view of Box Hill to the east, Ranmore Common, the Pilgrims' Way, and the railway running parallel to the downs.

When the lane meets the drive to Milton Court continue forward a few paces in the drive and turn right, so that the gatehouse is behind you and a mill pond on your left. When you are soon beside a semi-derelict barn on the right (with a house behind it) turn left. Then pass the left side of two open barns to an iron kissing-gate leading into a field. Don't be tempted into the track outside the left edge of the field but strike across the field to a stile about half way along, then straight on to another at the far end. You will notice that a stream follows the left edge of the field.

The second stile leads on to a short but firm track and to another stile at the far end. There is a crossing path just here and, later, a footbridge for access to the houses (Westcott) on the left. Ignore these and go forward to the next (concrete) footbridge, which also leads into Westcott (St John's Road). Do not cross the footbridge but turn right here – so that the footbridge is behind you – and cross the field to a stile: Then join a stony track heading straight up towards the downs.

Given good visibility you should see the tip of the spire of Sir Gilbert Scott's Ranmore Common church up on the downs – roughly half right as you proceed. Closer at hand on the hillside is an area of woodland called the 'Eyeglasses'. When you see it, you will know why!

Follow the track past Springfield House to a stile leading into a field, then along the field-edge to the far right-hand corner. Over a stream here as best you can and forward again beside an iron fence to the railway crossing. Straight on again and steeply uphill to the 'Denbies Coach Road' – the Pilgrims' Way once more. You should now turn right and continue from **(10)** on page 56; but before you do that, why not explore the Coach Road in the other direction? It is very nice down there!

Historical Notes

The Ordnance Survey map shows a short stretch of Pilgrims' Way situated about ½ mile north-east of Shere, coming from nowhere and going nowhere. I am tempted to attribute this to a cartographic slip of the pen! Having thus discounted this piece of 'evidence', it still remains difficult to define the correct route from Shere to Pickett's Hole (the steep combe below White Downs). So I hope we are excused when we map our own route on the basis of how pleasant and straightforward it is!

Shere is a picturesque village with many attractive cottages distributed around the Tillingbourne stream, but it has become a magnet to weekend walkers and motorists. So come out of season or during the week if you wish to avoid your own kind!

At the western end of the village you will find the Prison House, with overhanging upper storey. Once a jail it is now a private house. At the eastern end is St James' church with shingled spire (cedarwood tiles). Inside are some fragments of very early stained glass (14th century), 15th century brasses, and a small display of woodwind instruments originally used in the minstrels' gallery. On the north side of the church an anchorite cell is where, in 1329, Christine Carpenter was 'walled up' (seemingly at her own request, but I'm not convinced) for 'the fulfilment of a better life'. She received food through a grating on the outside, viewed the altar and received communion through small openings on the inside.

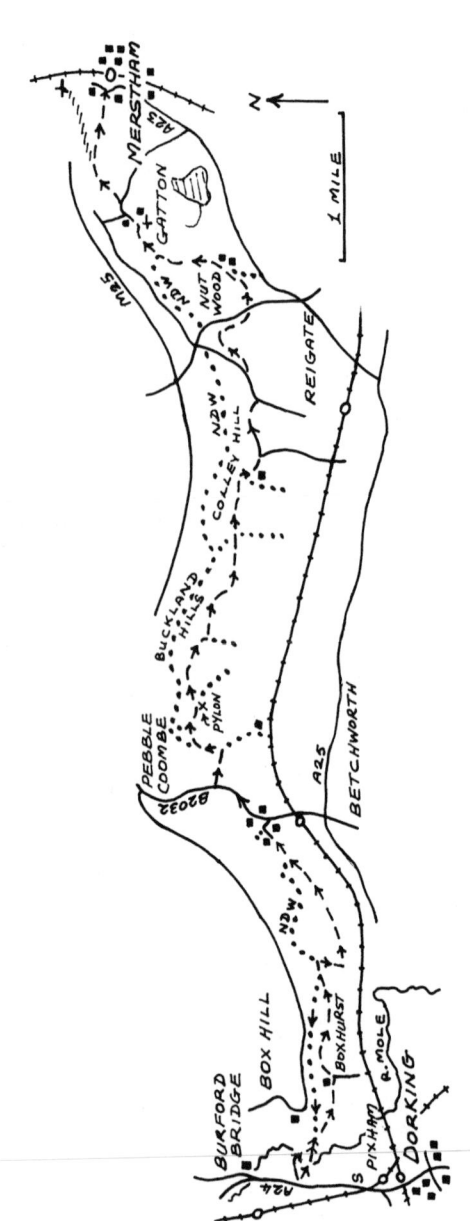

Dorking to Merstham

Introduction: An invigorating walk with superb views across the Greensand Hills. Fine stretches of chalk grassland along the lower contours of Buckland and Box Hills – with the glorious display of wild flowers and butterflies; the breathtaking expanse of Brockham chalk quarry, now disused and overgrown; the historical interest of Gatton Park and the sudden meeting with Merstham's Quality Street. A day to remember!

The circular walk starts at Dorking and returns from Brockham Hill, crossing the well-known summit of Box Hill.

Circular Walk: Dorking – Brockham Hill – Box Hill – Dorking
The walk is 4½ miles (7.3 km) and begins at Dorking Main Station. There is parking available in the old road adjacent to the A24, midway between the station and Burford Bridge.

Pilgrims' Route: Dorking to Merstham
The walk is 10 miles (16 km) and, like the circular walk, begins at Dorking main station.

To return to Dorking by public transport, there is a ½ hourly bus service (414/405) to Redhill (hourly on Sunday). From there a frequent rail service runs to Dorking Deepdene station.

The Walk: Turn right out of Dorking Station (the main line station; not Dorking West or Dorking Deepdene) and over the railway bridge on the A24. You will pass Pixham Lane and Boxlands on the right; then the start of the North Downs Way by a National Trust sign. Soon after joining the Way you are presented with a choice of crossings of the river Mole: the Stepping Stones or the footbridge (why not try both!)

The two routes join hands beyond the opposite bank of the river. Turn left if you have come from the bridge; keep straight on if from the stepping stones. The path climbs steeply, with a right curve, then

59

a left, giving a breathtaking view of the Mole. At the next right curve the path levels out briefly.

This is where your utmost powers of concentration must be brought to bear! Don't go forward along the uphill terraced path (the North Downs Way) but turn half right (150 degrees) towards a small concrete post marked 'DUDC' (Dorking Urban District Council) and join a level path that runs along the hillside. A field soon appears down on the right, with a warning to 'Keep Out', and a stile ahead leads onto the open grassland.

Follow the lower edge of the grassland, parallel with a line of yew trees on the right. At the far end the path turns right to a stile and gate under trees. Ignore a path coming down from the left just beyond the stile and continue ahead to a lane. Go left in this and uphill for about 30 yards to a path on the right opposite the entrance gate to Boxhurst. This path runs uphill parallel to the drive and with a field on the right.

There is a T-junction under trees ahead, with an iron gate on the left leading to a house. Turn right here and soon enter another stretch of chalk grassland, with a hedge on your right. Back again under the trees of the Dukes Plantation, the path is in due course joined by the North Downs Way as it comes in from the left, rear. Turn left into this if you are returning to Dorking on the circular route; then continue from page 62.

To continue the walk to Merstham keep straight on, firstly down a flight of steps, then right and steeply downhill from a T-junction (the North Downs Way is steeply uphill). Go all the way to an iron gate and stile at the bottom – beside a Second World War pill box. Turn left here into the level path just above the fields. Stay with this for $\frac{1}{3}$ mile until you pass above a row of houses (ex-quarry workers' houses, I imagine) to another iron gate. For a truly magnificent view of Brockham Quarry, now disused and overgrown, divert along a path that runs up from the gate.

Back at the gate continue forward into the open, passing old buildings and an equally old timber cottage, and immediately curve right to a stile (not the adjacent gate). As you meander your way along from the stile, never far above the fields, two paths slanting off to the left, and a crossing path, should be ignored.

In the fullness of time you will approach the vast expanse of Betchworth chalk quarry, with a tall ivy-clad tower in its midst. The path comes to an abrupt end here and you must go left and uphill to rejoin the North Downs Way after a few yards. Turn right in this and soon enjoy another view (by diverting through the trees on the right) of the tower and, 2 miles away, the windmill on Reigate Heath. The way ahead passes another quarry and a row of houses before joining a drive coming in from the left. Next port of call is the B2032 where you should turn left.

You must now suffer ½ mile of this busy road, but you have the protection afforded by a pavement and a footpath. When these end cross over to a tarmac path opposite – the North Downs Way. This straight and level path under trees eventually comes out into the open at a stile. Turn left here, cross another stile, and go uphill towards the downs. Looking back you have a particularly good view of the windmill.

Soon after entering the woods on the steep slope of the downs, go right at a fork in the path. You will remain more or less on the level until meeting a wide path coming in from the left. Go right with this and then follow its left curve – under yew trees and on a raised terrace – until you meet a T-junction near an electricity pylon. Turning left here you will soon be skirting the upper edge of cornfields and hopefully enjoying the lovely prospect of downland, chalk grassland and cultivated fields.

In less than ½ mile you will come to a Y-junction (not where a path comes in from the left, rear). Take the left-hand branch (with the yellow arrow) and go straight on at a crossing (where there are steps cut on the left). The next ¾ mile will find you bobbing in and out of the trees – with fields over to the right – eventually meeting a crossing track under yew trees.

You will be pleased to learn that you don't go uphill in that sunken, muddy, gloomy, uninviting piece of the North Downs Way (unless you so desire) but straight on in a wide, level path under yew trees. When this forks before the second of two combes, go down a flight of steps and pass anticlockwise around the combes in the main path. Go over a crossing and ahead to a fork – before a house called Broadleas.

Keep left here, so that the house and associated farm buildings are on your right. Before very long a gate will lead you into civilisation and forward in a road. When the road curves right near Under-beeches continue straight on along a bridleway running between a wall and a fence. This pleasant stretch terminates beyond the equally pleasant Coachman's Cottage, and less pleasant A217.

Go left in the A217 and branch right after about 200 yards into a bridleway signposted to Wray Lane. This soon becomes a level terraced path under trees, with fields on the right (Pilgrims' Way true to type!). The path curves right and follows a timber fence sheltering Wray Lane House. After joining a drive at Hunter's lodge, soon leave it by branching into a path to the right of Little Beeches and staying with it to a road.

Cross the road to National Trust land opposite and walk along the left side of a brick wall. When the wall soon ends turn right into a level path beside a timber fence. When this also comes to an end continue ahead in a meandering path under trees, with a field on the right. The path soon joins a wide track at a crossing. Turn right here and, with fields still on the right, keep straight on past two National Trust waymark posts and join a drive going forward into the open. You will have glimpses of Gatton Park and its modern outbuildings as you proceed.

Turn right in the main drive ahead and stay in this through the estate, with those modern buildings now on your right. Before going left with the drive at the assembly hall, a diversion to the church is well worthwhile, as is a discreet look at the House and the 'Town Hall' (see Historical Notes).

You will join a public road beyond North Lodge. Go forward in the road and, 30 yards after it curves right, join a drive on the left. This will lead you into a footpath and through a Pick Your Own fruit farm (and into temptation no doubt!). There is an unpleasant melee of 'M' and 'A' roads ahead as you make your way forward across fields, and to the left of a cricket green.

It is then a short run into Merstham, with Quality Street to greet you. For the station turn right into the A23, then first left. For the 'through route' turn left into Quality Street and continue from (11) on page 65.

Returning to Dorking from Brockham Hills: From the left-hand hairpin turn in the track, go uphill in the North Downs Way until a 'private' gate bars the way. Go left here down a flight of steps and, when these terminate, turn right and follow a long level path under trees, guided by acorn waymarks.

You will cross a sunken track (leading to the Smuggler's Rest and a tea garden) followed by a ditch. Once over the ditch the acorn waymarks will lead you left and parallel (at a distance) to a road. Stay with the acorns as you emerge onto the open hillside of Box Hill, passing to the left of an observation platform giving views of the windmill on Reigate Heath on the extreme left and Leith Hill Tower (at 210 degrees) amongst the trees on the southern horizon. Leith Hill is the highest point in South East England.

For the National Trust's tearoom, shop and information room go left in the road just above the platform. It is a short distance only, and well worthwhile.

Continuing forward from the observation platform along a well-used path you will soon arrive at a parting of the ways. Forward on the level for 200 yards for Peter Labelliere's grave (follow the red arrows) or downhill under a dark canopy of yew trees to finish the walk (follow the acorn waymarks). The latter will eventually place you on familiar ground as you descend to the crossing of the river Mole.

Historical Notes

Exactly where the Pilgrims' Way crossed the river Mole as it passed to the north of Dorking is not at all certain. Burford Bridge has been suggested as a possible site but this would have involved a marshy approach to the river and a long detour around Box Hill. A crossing at Pixham seems likely, since this conforms to the general alignment of the Way further east. Most people today would make use of the footbridge or stepping stones one mile north of Dorking. This is the crossing used by the North Downs Way – and by us.

It is curious that the Pilgrims' Way east of the river at Boxhurst is marked on the 1:100,000 Ordnance Survey map as being one and the same as a line of electricity pylons, but on the 1:50,000 map it has been moved up a little to coincide with a path on National Trust land! Since we have no desire to trudge across ploughed fields under electricity pylons we take the higher route running from the stepping stones at Boxland through Boxhurst to Brockham Hill.

The Way subsequently passes below Brockham chalk quarry (as do we) and crosses Betchworth Quarries before meeting the B2032 road north of Betchworth station.

The route of the Pilgrims' Way across Pebble Coombe (also north of Betchworth Station) and along the Buckland Hills is very much open to debate: whether it followed the crest of the hills or simply kept to the lower slopes. We take the latter course since this is a quiet, easy-going route through a lovely area of chalk grassland.

It is possible that the final ¾ mile descent into Merstham from Whitehall fruit farm followed a more direct route than the one currently in use. This would pass closer to Merstham church and would be in direct line with the Way east of Merstham.

Dorking: Your first encounter with old Dorking may well be along West Street with its many antique shops. West Street runs into High Street. Between them these two streets exhibit an interesting miscellany of building styles – including the inevitable supermarket with blank wall and glass. The town pump, now no more than a curiosity, holds aloft a road sign where the two streets meet. The church of St Martin calls our attention from innumerable vantage points. Its tall, slender spire is a memorial to Bishop Samuel Wilberforce, son of William Wilberforce who devoted the greater part of his life to the abolition of the slave trade. Inside, the church is sombre: the 'best work' of Henry Woodyer.

Box Hill: It may go without saying that the hill is named after the box trees that grow here in abundance. You may however be much more aware of the yew trees which cast their deep shadow over many of the footpaths. Box Hill, including 1,200 acres hereabouts, is protected by the National Trust. Their visitor centre, including a gift shop, information room and tearoom, is situated at the top of the hill close to the route of our circular walk.

Also close to our walk is the grave of Major Peter Labelliere 'an eccentric resident of Dorking' buried head downwards in July 1800. It was his own wish to be laid thus, so that when 'the trumpet shall sound' and everything turns topsy-turvy, he will be the right way up!

Gatton: To our democratic minds it seems strange that a community the size of Gatton – manor house, church and a few cottages, could send two Members to Parliament. That was before the Reform Act of 1832, when the exchange of large sums of money could ensure 'election'. The imposing pillared portico of Gatton House overlooks well manicured lawns to what must be the smallest and most unusual 'town hall' in existence. And the nearby church is a veritable museum of ecclesiastical art, with items – mostly in wood – collected from numerous sources in Europe.

Gatton is now home to the Royal Alexandra and Albert School for Deprived and Erring Children, hence the profusion of modern buildings across the estate.

Merstham to Oxted

Introduction: We take one long look at Merstham's Quality Street before quickly crossing two motorways and ascending Ockley Hill to the airy summit of the Downs. Then along pleasant level trackways to White Hill with views of London on the northern horizon. The path skirts Gravelly Hill on its way to the A22 and the beechwood heights of Tandridge Hill. There is a superb descent from Tandridge Hill before crossing the M25 and skirting the grounds of Barrow Green Court.

Circular Walk: Sadly there is no suitable circular route for this section.

Pilgrims' Route: Merstham to Oxted
The walk is 9 miles (14.5 km) and begins at Merstham railway station. There is parking available at the Village Hall nearby.
To return to Merstham by public transport, buses run hourly to Redhill Mon–Sat (410). From there bus service 414/405 runs ½ hourly to Merstham Mon–Sat, hourly on Sunday.

The Walk: For a short cut starting at Merstham railway station and avoiding the village (and the attractive Quality Street!), see page 69, otherwise from Merstham Station go along Station Road and turn right at the end into the A23. Leave the A23 when it curves right and go forward into Quality Street, a no through road. **(11)** Almost at the end of Quality Street, and just beyond the Old Forge (a Building of Special Interest) turn half-right into a path that soon crosses the M25 motorway. The path meets a road by the parish church, which will probably be locked. Turn right in this road and go down to the extremely busy A23. With great care cross to Rockshaw Road opposite and go along this and over two separated railway lines.
After the space of about 15 houses along Rockshaw Road a path

comes in from the right, bringing those who took the short-cut from Merstham Station. **(12)** Soon after this (150 yards), but on the left just before a knot of houses, a North Downs Way sign marks your exit from the road. A path will take you across a field and under the M23 (which is plunging headlong into a vast spaghetti junction with the M25).

From the M23, the path makes its way diagonally uphill, passing a barn on the left and heading for the top right-hand corner of a field. It cuts through a rank of trees and continues in the same direction to the top right-hand corner of another field, passing an overgrown quarry on the left. Looking back you will doubtless see aircraft landing at distant Gatwick Airport.

At the top of the hill you are joined by a track which takes you almost straight and level for about a mile – crossing Hilltop Lane and passing a number of desirable residences. At the end of that mile the Way, now a tarmac drive, passes Willey Park Farm and soon meets a lane coming up from the left. On a clear day you may be able to identify London landmarks on the horizon to the north.

Now don't go left into that lane but continue in the road, which soon turns right. A very pleasant stretch follows, before meeting Stanstead Road. As you cross to War Coppice Road opposite, The Harrow public house is nearby.

After about ½ mile of road you will pass Woodland Way and the entrance to War Coppice Lodge and, soon after that, the crossing with Weald Way and Hextalls Lane. Gravelly Hill rises steeply from the road on the left and is topped by aerial masts. A stile at the corner of Hextalls Lane will place you on a path under trees that diverges

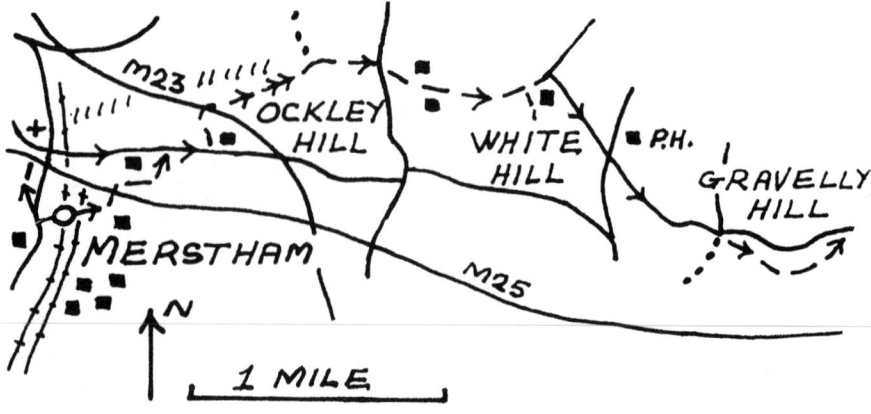

slightly from War Coppice Road. You will notice that the path runs along a terrace – a feature that often indicates an ancient route – and that there are at least two other terraced paths running parallel.

When one of these paths decides to go half right downhill you should continue ahead on the level. This will take you under some venerable yew trees and out into the open at a roadside picnic area with a view of the motorway lower down.

Where the road turns left and leaves the picnic area you should go right along a wide woodland track. This track rotates anticlockwise around a steep knoll, a knoll surmounted by Pilgrim Fort. If you take your cue from the acorn waymarks while ignoring other distractions (namely a path going off steeply from the right, and later a tinkers' caravan site) you will arrive at Tuckwood Lane, where you should turn right.

Just before the lane turns sharp left on its way down to the A22 and two fast-food caravans, you will find a path on the right leading to a footbridge over the A22.

From the footbridge go straight on across a field to a stile. Turn right here along a path under trees then half left over another stile after 100 yards, just beyond a transformer. Be sure you don't go straight on! You will soon be led down some steps to a drive that serves a small industrial complex. Cross to a path under trees opposite, and pass to the right of an unusual many-sided (I lost count!) office building. You will soon meet another drive, this one leading to a small car park.

Go right in the drive and follow it through as it runs along a terrace, firstly in the open and then left under trees. After about ⅓

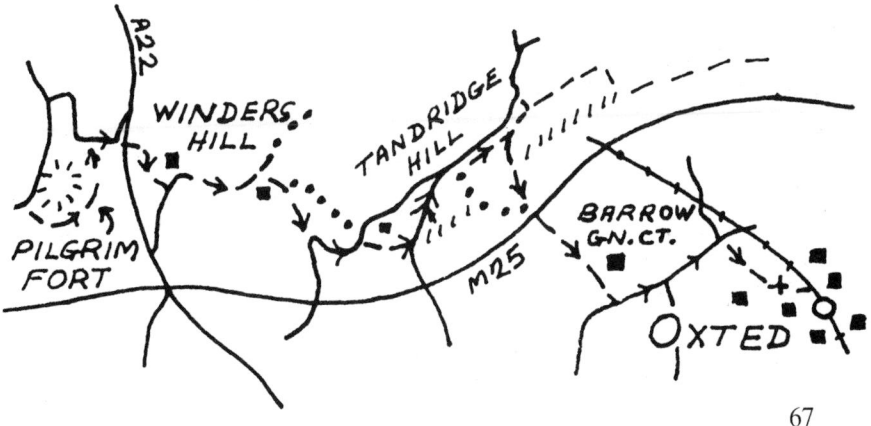

mile you will come up to a chalk-stone house, South Lodge, at a footpath junction. The pleasanter North Downs Way continues from a stile here but this rather scruffy stretch of the Pilgrims' Way is a level track leaving from the right. So you have a choice! The two ways meet up again at a road ¾ mile further on.

At the end of the track you will emerge at a hairpin bend in the aforementioned road. Now don't go happily on downhill, but left and uphill in the road. When the road turns left under trees you will meet the crossing of the North Downs Way. Rejoin this by turning right in a fenced path (not the earlier downhill bridleway) beside Hanging Wood Forest Farm.

This narrow path drops down to within one blade of grass of a lane. The Pilgrims' Way originally went straight on from here (in effect across the lane and into the field opposite) but there is now no right of access. Instead go left over a stile and follow a path running uphill, parallel to the lane.

Soon after the path joins the lane at the top of the hill, turn right at a T-junction. Go along the road for about 75 yards to where a path goes downhill from the right. This is a wet and muddy route to Oxted, so we shall ignore it! Continue ahead but just inside the wood and parallel to the road. Stay like this for ⅓ mile until you see an 'S-bend' sign on the road to your left.

For the through route continue from (13) on page 72. For Oxted your full powers of concentration are again required! Just before you come level with the 'S-bend' road sign you should be able to find a path doubling back through the trees on your right. It starts 50 yards back from a flight of steps linking the path you are now on with the road opposite a small car park.

The required path runs gradually downhill under trees (140 degrees at the start, 180 later) just above the steep edge of the hillside. After 100 yards it drops briefly and steeply down, but soon resumes its previous direction. After 30 more yards it divides into two. You should keep straight on here, down a clear chalky path through an area of scrubland.

The dividing line between the hawthorn woodland and the less steep pastures lower down is where the Pilgrims' Way once passed on its near-level course.

Follow the path over this line and straight on downhill to a stile and gate. Cross the M25 to a track which eventually passes the entrance to Barrow Green Court. This heavily fortified 17th century manor house is said to be 'one of the most interesting of its kind in East

Surrey'. From our restricted view much of it appears to be 20th century! The drive meets a T-junction with a road, where you should turn left.

Ignore the first turning on the right and continue on to a three-way road junction. Take the Oxted branch (straight on) and turn right into a bridleway after 40 yards. This will lead you between fields to Oxted church. There are three ways into Oxted itself: the shortest by a foot or two is by turning right and walking through the old churchyard to Bluehouse Lane, then into Station Approach.

Short-cut from Merstham station to Rockshaw Road: From the south-going platform join a footpath that leads to Malmstone Avenue. Go forward in the road for 100 yards to a footpath on the left. This will take you at right-angles to the road and to a footbridge over the M25. From here the well-used path goes right then left, ascending the hill to Rockshaw Road by a house called Oakwood. Turn right in the road and continue from **(12)** on page 66.

Historical Notes

Hilaire Belloc, writing in 1904, was 'fairly certain' that the Pilgrims' Way climbed to the crest of the downs diagonally from Merstham, his evidence being a 'continuous alignment of yew, hedge and track' coming straight up from the parish church. The difficulties that men and animals would have experienced in traversing the steep escarpment east of Merstham made it necessary to follow this 'second best' route, which placed them on the level summit and kept them there for at least as long as the steepness prevailed. The railway and motorway prevent us from following Belloc's hypothetical approach to the summit, so we walk instead along Rockshaw Road before 'underpassing' the M23 and ascending the downs.

One mile of Pilgrims' Way running north-east from Tandridge Hill near Oxted is equally inaccessible. Its line follows the lower edge of some old quarries, in an area of scrub and grassland owned by the National Trust, and crosses the portals of Oxted railway tunnel. Since there is no right-of-way along here our route follows the North Downs Way along the summit of the hill.

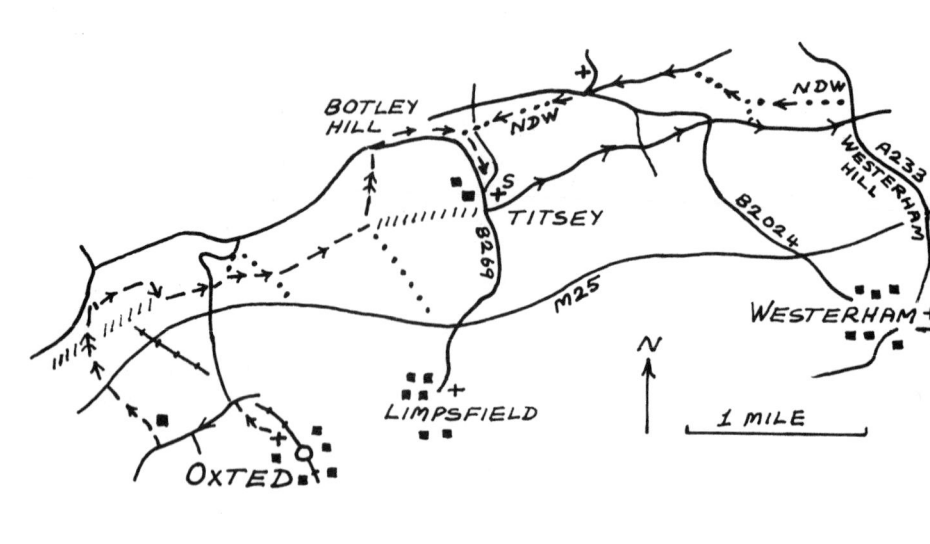

BOTLEY
HILL

NDW

+S

TITSEY

B2269

NDW

WESTERHAM
HILL

A233

B2024

M25

WESTERHAM

LIMPSFIELD

N

1 MILE

OXTED

Oxted to Westerham Hill

Introduction: From Oxted it is a 2 mile walk to join the summit of the Downs above the impressive slopes of Tandridge Hill. From this high point the path descends in stages, each time levelling out along lovely stretches of chalk grassland and cultivated fields. As if by an after-thought the route soon strikes steeply up to Botley Hill, only to descend again to Titsey. From Titsey the Pilgrims' Way is a delightful country lane 4½ miles in length. Westerham Hill is reached after two of these miles and is the turning point for Westerham itself.

The circular walk leaves the route at Westerham Hill and takes to higher ground, making full use of the well-marked North Downs Way back to Titsey.

Circular Walk: Titsey – Westerham Hill – Betsom's Hill – Titsey
The walk is 5 miles (8 km) and starts at **(14)** on page 73 at St James' Church at Titsey. There is parking available in the layby opposite the church.

Pilgrims' Route: Oxted to Westerham Hill
The walk is 7 miles (11.3 km) and begins at Oxted station. There is a convenient car park east of the station off Amy Road.

To return to Oxted by public transport, buses run hourly Mon–Sat only (410).

The Walk: Leave Oxted Station from the platform One side and turn right into Station Approach. At the end of this road turn left into Bluehouse Lane and cross a T-junction towards the church. A path across the old graveyard will lead you past the church to an iron gate on the far side. Now don't cross over to the 'No Cycling' path opposite but turn right to follow the churchyard wall and soon left into a path beside the new graveyard. You then have ¼ mile of fenced path across fields to a road.

Go left in the road and straight on at a T-junction in the Godstone direction. Ignore a turning on the left after ¼ mile and look for a drive on the right just beyond fortified Barrow Green Court (see page 68). This drive passes a tradesman's entrance to the Court and eventually, as a track, crosses the M25. Branch right at a stile and gate just beyond the M25, then go uphill across a field, passing a solitary oak tree and aiming for a chalky path higher up. In due course you will reach a stile in the lower border of an area of trees and scrub.

The Pilgrims' Way originally passed along this border on a level route. Since this stretch is not a right-of-way you are constrained to pass it by and continue uphill, now more steeply and in a chalky path, until you meet a T-junction with another path under trees.

Turn right at the T-junction and follow the narrow path diagonally uphill (30 degrees initially, then zero degrees and including a short uphill section) until you meet a wide path (the North Downs Way) under trees just below a road. Turn right and (13) follow the wide path parallel to the road for 50 yards until you see a flight of steps ascending to the road.

Don't climb the steps but go forward a few yards and turn right down a very steep path. You will have a unique view of the railway line heading straight for Oxted, and your steep descent will be terminated when a stile on the left leads you on to a level path. You will soon be out in the open on a lovely stretch of chalk downland, adorned in summer with the brightness of butterflies and wild flowers.

The line of the Pilgrims' Way (the part that is not a right-of-way) crosses the cultivated fields lower down – a barn lying directly on the route. You will soon join the accessible extension to this by turning right at a 'National Trust Oxted Downs' sign and descending the hill.

Go well downhill to a signpost and turn left across the centre of a field, eventually following its top left-hand edge. A large quarry is part hidden by trees on the left. If you keep more or less straight on you will meet up with a short path passing to the right of two houses and leading to a road. Go right in the road for 35 yards and left into a hillside path from a stile. Branch left from the next stile quite soon and go uphill in a chalky path to another stile on the right, labelled with the acorn waymark. This will place you on a level route along the top edge of a field, with hawthorn scrub left.

There is a National Trust sign at the end of the field, and two stiles that lead you forward. You now have ⅔ mile of a straight and level path just below the Titsey Plantation (see Historical Notes), after which take a left turn and go steeply uphill through the plantation. Earlier pilgrims were more fortunate as they could continue on the level to Titsey – at least until the Way was closed to the public many years ago.

As you climb the hill an excellent view of Titsey Park can be enjoyed by diverting a short distance along a path on the right – a path open to the public.

If you have any strength left on arrival at the top of the hill you should go sharp right into the B269 (for Oxted) at the road junction. With the traffic as fast as it is here, you will need no encouragement to walk along the footpath in the trees on the left. This starts at the top of the hill and follows the road all the way down to Titsey church – or very nearly. You should ignore a branch in the path (the North Downs Way) going off left about half-way down.

(14) A left turn into the Pilgrims' Way just beyond the church marks the start of the circular walk and takes you past Church Cottage and Forge Cottage. The latter has three types of construction – timber-frame, flint, and clunch (chalk stone). You then have a 2 mile stretch of quiet country lane to Westerham Hill on the A233. This will involve keeping straight on at two slightly staggered crossings, the second being the B2024 on the Surrey–Kent boundary. It is a right turn into the A233 followed by a mile or so into Westerham, on foot or by bus (route 410, hourly Mon–Sat only). For the circular walk turn left into the A233 and continue thus:

Returning to Titsey from Westerham Hill: From the Pilgrims' Way go uphill in the A233 for 100 yards to The Avenue on the left. This is the North Downs Way and soon becomes a rough track going uphill through the trees. Some very fine residences accompany the Way, and the surface eventually reverts to tarmac.

When the Way meets a T-junction by a letter-box turn left, enjoy the fine views over the Weald, covet yet more six-figure residences, and continue to a junction with the B2024. While you are here, do have a look at Tatsfield church. This is just a short distance uphill from the B2024.

Cross the B2024 to the south side and join a path (still the North Downs Way) down steps and under trees to a stile. Turn right from the stile and follow the top edge of the fields parallel to the road. After passing a farmhouse and crossing the next stile the route diverges from the road by going slightly left and slightly downhill.

Oxted and its silvered gasometer will be almost directly ahead before a stile takes you into a wood. Where a lane interrupts the wood you should continue ahead – eventually to meet two stiles. From the second stile there is a short, steep descent to a T-junction with another path. Turn left here (leaving the North Downs Way) and go downhill parallel to the B269 road. This will take you back to Titsey.

Historical Notes

Our route from Oxted to the crest of the Downs crosses a private stretch of the Pilgrims' Way. Since there is no public right-of-way here or across Titsey Park 2 miles further on, we are constrained to take alternative routes.

Oxted: As you approached Oxted from the Downs yesterday you were welcomed first of all by a view of the parish church. On arrival you may have noticed that the church was placed within a circular graveyard, an interesting feature which suggests that the site was occupied by primitive man – a stone circle perhaps. Beyond the church pseudo-Tudor commuterland is pleasant, friendly and seemingly complete. Take time to explore the old village with its 16th century buldings, its lock-up, and its pound.

Limpsfield is a picturesque village ¾ mile north-east of Oxted. The High Street, which includes a number of 15th century hall-houses, is a Conservation Area. One of the hall-houses, Detillens, is open to the public. Among the notable persons buried at St Peter's church is the composer Frederick Delius, who died in 1934.

Titsey: Titsey Place is tucked away behind a screen of estate trees, out of sight of our route. The house was built in 1775 and 'altered for the worse' in 1832. It is not open to the public. The Titsey plantation is part of the 4,000 acre estate and was created between 1807 and 1840 when some half million trees were planted. A 4 mile walk has been laid out through the plantation for use by the public.

St James' church at the crossroads is the fourth in a succession of churches to be built here at Titsey, each one replacing the one before. The first two (Saxon and Norman) were on a site near the present Titsey Place. The third 'ugly and uncomfortable' church was replaced in 1860. A notice board announces that this fourth church has 'many historical features' and that restoration and maintenance is in the hands of the Titsey Charitable Foundation.

Westerham Hill to Otford

Introduction: This walk offers two miles of unmolested Pilgrims' Way road at its very best, with superb views of the Downs on the one hand, and the Kentish Weald on the other. Beyond these two miles further progress along the Way is halted owing to its enclosure within Chevening Park, but steep (very steep!) Sundridge Hill is a diversion that connects with a right-of-way through the Park. The reward for this uphill effort is a lovely walk in open woodland with fine views of Chevening House and the surrounding countryside. Beyond Chevening a short, close encounter with the M25 must be endured before rejoining the Pilgrims' Way and walking the final 2½ miles to Otford.

The circular walk takes advantage of the North Downs Way for the return route from Sundridge Hill along lanes and field edges and back to Westerham Hill.

Circular Walk: Westerham Hill – Sundridge Hill – North Downs Way – Westerham Hill
The walk is 6½ miles (10.5 km) and begins one mile north of Westerham (grid reference 441558). There is parking space on a wide grass verge beside the A233 very near the Pilgrims' Way path where the walk begins.

Pilgrims' Route: Westerham Hill to Otford
The walk is 8 miles (13 km) and begins at the same point as the circular walk, above.

Unfortunately there is no convenient public transport to return to Westerham Hill, but a list of taxi services is given at the end of the book.

The Walk: From the A233 go into the clearly marked Pilgrims' Way – a country lane – with Betsoms Farm house on the right initially (not the barns, which are on the opposite side of the A233). This is a right turn if approaching from Westerham. You should see the M25 ¾ mile away on your right.

75

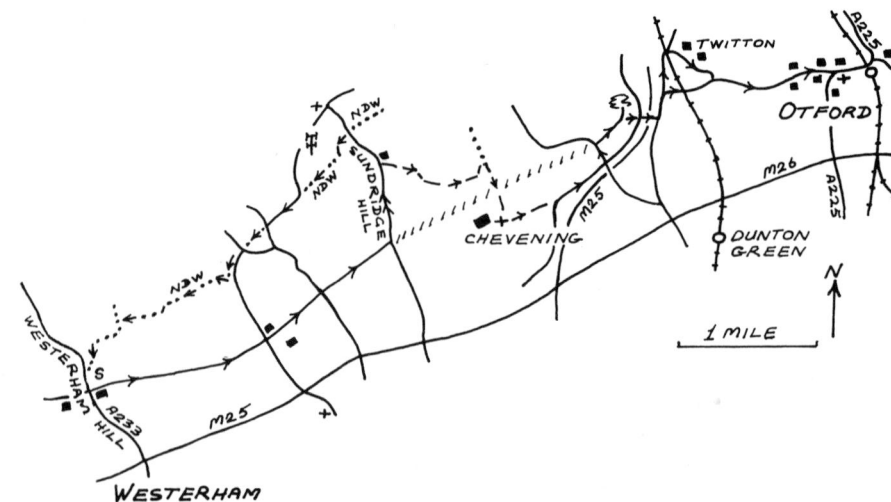

WESTERHAM

Now it is a very pleasant but uneventful mile or so to the first road crossing by Hogtrough Cottage, where you should keep straight on (for Sundridge).

Cross the road to continue on the Pilgrims' Way, or more correctly go right a few paces then left. Two-thirds of a mile of this lovely quiet road will take you to a T-junction. The Pilgrims' Way continues straight on through an iron gate into the Chevening Estate but there has been no right of access here since the 3rd Earl Stanhope closed it to the public in 1792. So there is no choice but to go left up Sundridge Hill. After ¾ mile of this very steep hill you will find Keeper's Cottage, with interesting tiling. If you are on the circular walk continue from page 78.

To continue the linear walk turn right into a path just before the cottage. Having done that go straight on through Park Wood, ignoring a gate on the right after about 100 yards. The path turns half right (ignore the branch on the left here) and Chevening House soon comes into view, as does the true line of the Pilgrims' Way at the bottom of the hill. Keeping close to the wood on the left, go downhill finally to an iron gate at the end of a short piece of farm track. Don't go through the gate but into the field on the right just before it, and follow a wire fence downhill to a drive. And don't go wandering off towards the House for a better view (as I did) or you may be interviewed by the constabulary (as I was!). Some maps do show a

76

path leading in that direction but the right-of-way has now been extinguished.

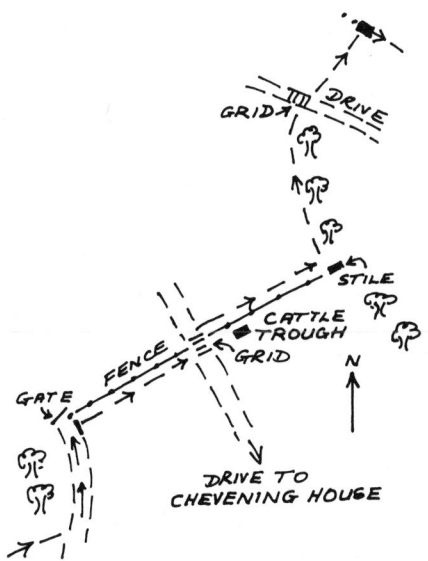

Continue in the same direction from the drive but by first crossing a cattle grid. Following the left side of a wire fence and passing a cattle trough you will soon reach a stile in the far corner of a field. Without going over that stile turn left and follow the remnant of a line of trees to another stile. Cross a drive here, to the right of a cattle grid, and go straight on across a field to a stile at a T-junction.

Go right here along a narrow path between fields to Chevening church. Enter the churchyard and turn left at a junction of paths. Then leave the churchyard on the east side after passing a memorial cross and go straight on along a grassy path. This will take you past a new graveyard, then along a narrow path and straight on to the B2211 road, at a bend. Go forward in the road for ½ mile to a roundabout, passing two farms on the left, ignoring any North Downs Way signs that you may see.

From the roundabout turn left into Starhill Road, then first right into Lime Pit Lane – the Pilgrims' Way once more! At the end of the lane, there are no less than four exits – one track and three drives. Take the right-hand of the three drives; the 'Private, Keep Out' signs don't apply to you! Go through a waymarked gate, and follow the drive to its end beyond two concrete bollards. Cross the A224 and the M25 and turn left at a T-junction into Pilgrims' Way West. This road curves right and will take you into Otford without further ado.

However, since this is a busy road and there is no verge or pavement for a short distance on either side of the railway bridge, I suggest that you divert through the attractive hamlet of Twitton. For this turn first left, then right into Twitton Lane after crossing the railway. Turn left when you reach the busy road again.

Returning to Westerham Hill from Sundridge Hill: From Keeper's Cottage continue uphill to where the wood on the right thins out. The North Downs Way crosses the road here and use is made of this route (with its acorn waymarks) all the way back to Westerham Hill.

Turn left at a stile into the Way and follow the left edge of a field to its corner, with the road just over the hedge on your left. Turn right from the corner and follow an apology for a hedge on the left. The road will now be behind you; also a stile well-hidden in the roadside hedge. From the far end of the hedge go forward into a large field ahead (radio masts in view half-right) and turn left to follow its hedge. Turn right when you are in the field's corner, placing the radio masts half-right again.

With that complicated manoeuvre out of the way, you should now be following a long, wide stand of trees, with good views through the storm-damage breaks, including Sevenoaks. The large white house beyond the M25 is Combe Bank, a girls convent school. At the end of this long wood you can either go forward in the lane or in the adjacent field on the left. The field route is rough going, and not my first choice.

At a T-junction in the lane signposted Bradsted, Cudham and Knockholt go forward over a stile (not through the adjacent gate) and into a level path along the right-hand edge of a field, following a line of trees on the right. The next road junction is a mirror image of the first. Cross to a stile opposite and walk along the field edge, with the road running parallel on the left but mostly out of sight.

Go over a stile at the end of the second field. There is an iron gate here and a North Downs Way plinth bidding you turn right towards a wood at the top edge of a field. Turn left just inside the wood, follow the path to a stile, and continue forward past a superior residence and swimming pool to a stile on the left (the path turns right just here). Cross the stile and revert to your forward direction, along the right-

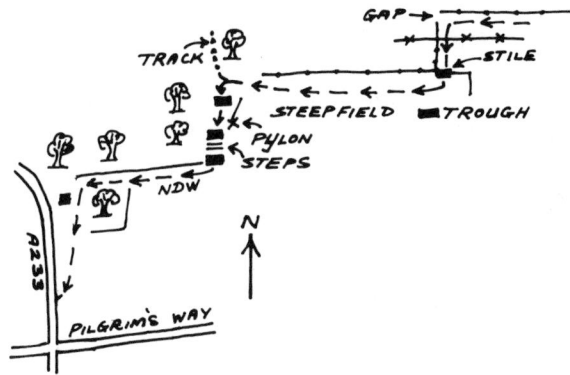

hand edge of a meadow. Then go over three stiles (all in one place!) and past a cattle trough.

Now be careful not to go forward through a gap in the far right-hand corner of the field you are now in. It is a natural thing to do, I know! Instead turn left under electricity wires and with a hedge on the right go down to the corner of the field. Continue forward a few yards to a stile and cattle trough at the top edge of a steep field. Westerham is in view ahead, also the M25.

Cross the stile and turn right, then follow the top edge of the field, with a wood on the right. Join a track in the far right-hand corner and go along this through trees to where it turns right. Don't go right with it, but left through scrub and trees to a stile; then straight on downhill to a stile beyond an electricity pylon. Pass through more trees and scrub, descending steps to another stile.

Turn right after that stile and go along the top edge of a field to another, hidden, stile in the far corner. Straight on again under trees and eventually left to pass a house on the right, with the A233 road behind it. You will soon enter a field, with a hedge and the A233 on the right. A stile will place you on the road opposite The Avenue, north of Betsomhill Farm.

Historical Notes

Westerham: This pleasant market town is noted for its association with a cavalcade of famous people, including Sir Winston Churchill, General Wolfe, William Pitt, and Andy Pandy! Chartwell Manor,

2 miles south of Westerham, was purchased by Sir Winston in 1922, and became his home until his death in 1965. It is one of the National Trust's most visited properties.

Also in the care of the National Trust is Quebec House, the boyhood home of Major-General James Wolfe. He was born at Westerham Vicarage in 1727 and followed a military career which, as victor in the Battle of Quebec, led to his death at the age of 32. Quebec House is near the junction of the A25 and B2026, east of the town.

William Pitt also excelled in early life, becoming Prime Minister in 1783 at the age of 24. He lived for a time in High Street, in a house now known as Pitt's Cottage. Luke Hansard (1752–1828) who initiated the printing of parliamentary proceedings now known as the Hansard Report, lived locally. Another local resident was Nissen, designer of the Nissen Hut. Andy Pandy, the television puppet, was created in a kitchen near Chartwell!

Chevening: Our right-of-way does not allow us to come closer than ¼ mile from the front of Chevening House, but the view at this distance is impressive enough. The central building was constructed around 1625, apparently to the design of Inigo Jones. A hundred years later the house was extended to include the two side wings, east and west of a courtyard. This was when a succession of Earls of Stanhope began their ownership, which lasted for more than 200 years.

It was the 3rd Earl who, in 1792, closed the Pilgrims' Way where it passed through the estate. In contrast, the 7th Earl gave the whole estate to the nation in 1959, not for public use, but as a kind of Chequers. Both Lord Hailsham and Prince Charles have resided here, but it is now the official home of the Foreign Secretary.

As you pass through St Botolph's churchyard on the walk it is interesting to see the humble graves of members of the Stanhope family. Their predecessors, the Lennards, rest more grandly inside the church.

Otford to Wrotham

Introduction: A fine stretch of Pilgrims' Way linking three jewels of Kent – Otford, Kemsing and Wrotham. Except for the last two miles into Wrotham the Way is a level country road accompanied for some distance by a parallel path under trees or behind hedges. Where the road turns south beyond St Clere, a 17th century mansion, the Pilgrims' Way continues ahead as a superb grassy track below the downs.

This is also the turning point for the circular route which heads steeply uphill, following the North Downs Way back to Hildenborough Hall. The descent from the Hall to Kemsing must be walked to be believed!

Circular Walk: Kemsing – St Clere – North Downs Way – Kemsing The walk is 4½ miles (7.3 km) and starts at **(15)** on page 82, in Kemsing village. There is a convenient car park near the Edith Hall.

Pilgrims' Route: Otford to Wrotham
The walk is 5½ miles (9 km) and starts at Otford station. Car parking is available in High Street.

To return to Otford by public transport, there is a ½ hourly train service Mon–Fri, hourly Sat–Sun, from Borough Green station. This is one mile south of Wrotham on the A227.

The Walk: From Otford station go over the railway bridge to the road junction. Turn right here into Pilgrims' Way East. This is a busy stretch of the Way, but relief is at hand. Ignore the North Downs Way path leaving from the left and the road going to Otford Manor called Row Dow (also ignore a school drive). Just prior to Beechy Lees Road you will find a path on the left running parallel with the road – the promised relief.

Now if you stay as close to the road as possible by keeping right at every junction in the path and straight on at a final three-way fork you will eventually renew contact with the road – at an entrance drive just beyond The Chase. If all this sounds too risky you could simply stay in the road!

Back in the road along a pleasant stretch of suburbia as far as the junction with Childsbridge Lane, where you should continue straight on. It is a quiet road now but you might prefer the parallel path behind the hedge on the left if only for the view (approach from the drive opposite Childsbridge Lane). Otford Manor (Hildenborough Hall on the map) stands on the crest of the downs. Once the home of Sir Oliver Lyle of Tate and Lyle, the house is presently the headquarters of Oak Hall Expeditions, a Christian holiday organisation.

The path rejoins the road at a turning called the Landway. The Pilgrims' Way is straight on. Immediately after a terrace of council-type houses called Pilgrims' Way Cottages, a path runs downhill to Kemsing.

Kemsing is an attractive village and you will not regret making the short diversion. (15) For those starting out on the circular route, this same path may be used to reach the Pilgrims' Way from the village. Entry to the path at the village end is where High Street joins West End.

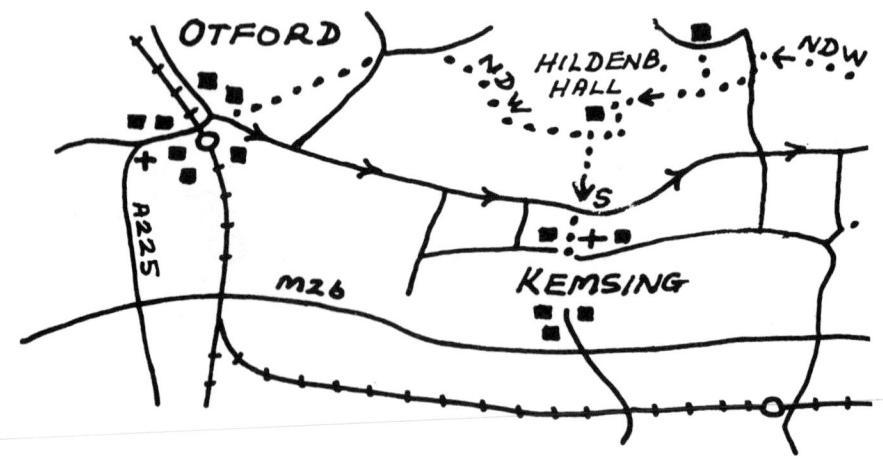

From the top of the path continue along the Pilgrims' Way, a quiet lane, passing soon the entrance drive to Kemsing Youth Hostel. After this the Way follows an extensive, well-groomed park, with seats conveniently placed. (If you wish, you can avoid the lane by walking forward just inside the park. When the border of the park curves away to the right, continue straight on along a path through trees, eventually to rejoin the lane just before Brushwood Cottage.) Three-quarters of a mile beyond the next road crossing you will pass a fine 17th century mansion, St Clere.

Ignore the turning on the left to West Kingsdown and continue in the lane until it goes into a hairpin right-hand turn. Wrotham VHF radio mast is in view on the left, at about one mile. The hairpin bend is the turning-point for the circular walk: for this continue from page 84.

To continue on the Pilgrims' Way to Wrotham, go forward into a track from the hairpin, ignoring a North Downs Way plinth on the left as you proceed. The track assumes the same west–east alignment as the lane, not surprisingly, since both are the Pilgrims' Way!

You will pass a wood on the left after ½ mile, before crossing a road. Now your inclination to go through the gate directly opposite is

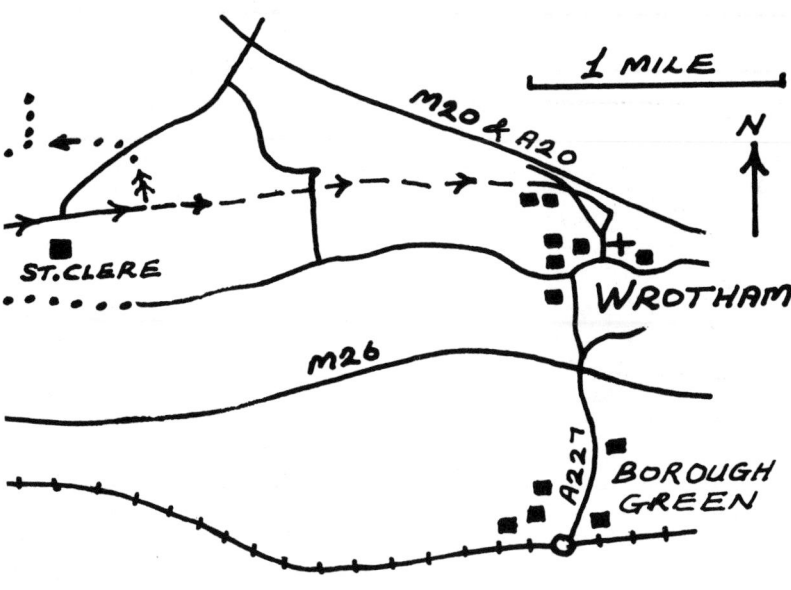

83

understandable, since there is a clearing ahead. However, the Pilgrims' Way continues slightly to the right of this, along a narrow path between hedges.

In less than a mile the narrow path meets a housing estate at Blacksole Field. The crossing just beyond this is Old London Road, now decapitated by the M20. Turn right in this for Wrotham. If you are staying on the Pilgrims' Way, cross the road opposite, and follow this round to the right where it joins the North Downs Way beyond a tennis court. Continue from (16) on page 87.

Returning to Kemsing from St Clere: From the hairpin bend go forward into a track (the Pilgrims' Way) and join a path on the left after a few yards. This is the North Downs Way, which will take you most of the way back to Kemsing, aided by acorn waymarks. Start by going uphill at right-angles to the Pilgrims' Way across a field to a stile, then slightly left and steeply uphill across another field to a stile near the top corner. A flight of steps will then place you on a road, where you should turn right.

Leave the road after 30 man-size paces and join a sloping path under trees on the left. Follow the path as it soon curves round to the left and uphill, then through the wood to a pedestrian gate. Fields then appear on the right while the wood remains on the left. The level path will take you past an old flint-lined pond; then along the right-hand edge of a field and over a crossing track. It follows the right-hand edge of another field and enters Summeryards Wood at the far end. The path will take you through the wood and along the right-hand edge of yet another field. Two cattle troughs appear on the right, and farm buildings ahead.

You will pass the farm on your right just before a road. Turn left in the road and go downhill for about 100 yards to a drive on the right marked 'Kester'. Go along the drive and join a path on the right after about 200 yards. The path runs into a field and goes forward along its left-hand edge. At the time of writing an alternative but unofficial route for the North Downs Way from the road to the field has been marked out. Strictly speaking this should be ignored. (A stile in the field's far right-hand corner marks the start of a ¼ mile path to the Rising Sun public house.)

Enter the wood ahead and emerge at the far end alongside a large pasture, with the wood extending on your left. At the far left-hand corner of the pasture follow 150 yards of wide track. A stile on the left at the far end takes you southerly to another stile. From that second stile cross a pasture half-left to its far left-hand corner. Then turn right (westerly again) along the hillside, with a magnificent panorama over the Weald of Kent. We have been skirting the outbuildings and gardens of Otford Manor (Hildenborough Hall), seen earlier from the Pilgrims' Way.

At the crossing path ahead take a left turn downhill to Kemsing, leaving the North Downs Way behind, or a right turn uphill for a view of the Hall. If you will also venture forward a few yards you will be rewarded with a fine view of the chalk downland above Kemsing.

When you have descended to the Pilgrims' Way above Kemsing you will doubtless recognise the path between Pilgrim Cottages and the Youth Hostel. This path will take you back to the village.

Historical Notes

Otford: I never cease to delight in the view from the London train as it races down the Darent Valley towards Otford. Motorists also come this way before inflicting noise and speed on this attractive village.

Apart from the walls of a row of adjoining cottages all that remains of Archbishop Warham's Tudor palace of 1515 is a three-storey ruined tower in view from the village pond. If the dimensions 440 ft by 220 ft fail to give some impression of the original extent of the palace, the fact that 'locks and keys for nearly 200 chambers' went missing in 1573 certainly will!

Kemsing: The heart of Kemsing is but a short footpath away from the Pilgrims' Way. Old cottages, a post office and a variety of trees overlook the tiny green, where St Edith's Well is adorned with seasonal flowers. St Edith was a nun and the daughter of the Saxon king, Edgar the Peaceful. Her brief lifespan covered but 24 years, from AD 961 to AD 984. Because of the miracles that could apparently be performed through her intercession, Kemsing naturally became a rendezvous for pilgrims travelling along the Way.

The church has many notable features including a shingled tower (wooden tiles), a 15th century porch and a lancet window with stained glass dating from 1220 – 'one of the treasures of the church'. The colourful chancel is complemented by a richly carved screen and a magnificent altar canopy. An intriguing 'crinkle crankle' wall alongside the churchyard adds the final touch to this pleasant diversion from the Pilgrims' Way. Was it built like that for strength, or to provide protection for crops or beehives?

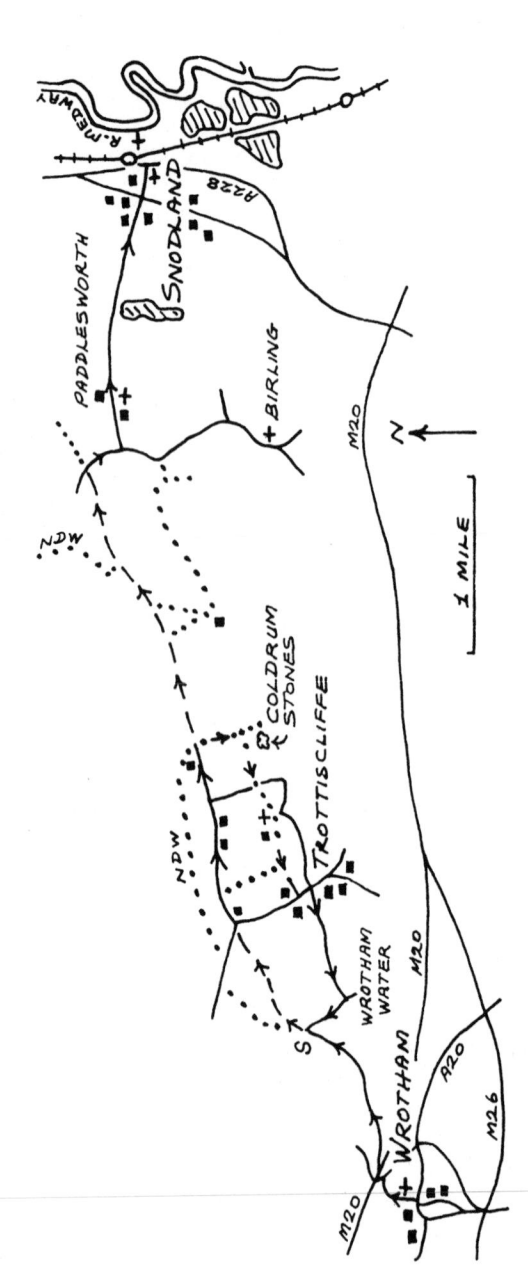

Wrotham to Snodland

Introduction: This is a very pleasant walk indeed. After crossing the M20, the Pilgrims' Way alternates between narrow country roads and ancient trackway, sometimes going with the North Downs Way, sometimes not.

In addition to an exceptional piece of Pilgrims' Way above Wrotham Water, the circular route includes a stop at the Coldrum Stones – a Stone Age long barrow of great interest. The route also passes Trottiscliffe church in its lovely rural setting, and Trottiscliffe itself – a picturebook Kentish village.

Circular Walk: Wrotham – Coldrum Stones – Trottiscliffe – Wrotham
The walk is 4½ miles (7.3 km) and starts at **(17)** on page 88, one mile from the M20 near Wrotham Water (grid reference 629597). There is parking here and where the road bends above Wrotham Water (grid reference 626602) near the Pilgrims' Way path, where the walk begins.

Pilgrims' Route: Wrotham to Snodland
The walk is 7 miles (11.3 km) and starts at St George's Church, Wrotham. There is a car park nearby in West Street.

To return to Wrotham by public transport, a train service runs to Maidstone Barracks ½ hourly Mon–Sat, hourly on Sunday. Then from Maidstone East station a ½ hourly service runs to Borough Green, one mile from Wrotham on the A227, hourly on Sunday.

The Walk: From St George's church go uphill and take the right-hand branch at a Y-junction (the other branch is the Old London Road). After passing a cricket green go right into the North Downs Way **(16)**, a tarmac path opposite a tennis court. Walk along this and you are soon deposited back into the 20th century as you enter the A20. Turn left and over the M20 to a roundabout and join the clearly marked Pilgrims' Way from the third exit.

The intrusive motorway noise soon fades as you make your way along this lane. Ignore North Downs Way signs enticing you into fields on the left; also Nepicar Lane on the right. Continue forward to a hairpin bend, Wrotham Water Road, one mile since crossing the M20.

(17) Leave the road here and go forward into a rough track labelled The Pilgrims' Way. After a few yards the North Downs Way makes its departure on the left. The Pilgrims' Way is straight on and it is a very pleasant ¾ mile to the road at Vigo Hill.

Turn right in the road and forward into a 'no-through-road' after passing Pilgrim House. This lane is accompanied by a path running parallel just inside the wood. I prefer the lane myself as there is more light and the view is better, including Trottiscliffe church in its delightful setting.

Pinesfield Lane comes in from the right, ¾ mile from Pilgrim House. Continuing straight on you will encounter a timber-clad cottage, Commority, on the left. A few steps beyond this, on the right, a ½ mile footpath leads down to the Coldrum Stones (see Historical Notes). This path is also the turning-point for those on the circular route – who should continue from page 89.

Back on the Pilgrims' Way (now a path and joined by the North Downs Way) the view across the Medway Valley opens up more and more, with Reeds huge paper factory in pride of place. After ¾ mile there is an old brick-built structure where a path comes in from the left, beyond which an enormous beech tree serves as a seat! About 130 yards after this keep left at a Y-junction, as directed by North Downs Way signs (the other branch goes down to Park Farm). At a crossing of paths ahead the North Downs Way takes its leave by turning left at a stile. Ignoring crossing paths continue straight on for ½ mile to a road.

Turn right in the road, passing an old quarry immediately, and first left for Snodland. The road will take you through Paddlesworth, a small settlement with ancient roots and its own, now disused, church. For the railway station go along High Street, over the A228 bypass, and then left. If you are continuing to Aylesford and beyond, turn right into Brook Street after crossing the A228 and continue from (18) on page 91.

Returning to Wrotham Water Road from the Coldrum Stones: Having come down the ½ mile path from the Pilgrims' Way to the Coldrum Stones, double back 90 paces from the Stones (facing the downs) and join a path leading into a field on the left. This path crosses the field parallel to the downs and soon passes through 'horsey' country to a road crossing. Go over the road to a stile and downhill to Trottiscliffe church (see Historical Notes).

With the church on your right go through the farmyard and along a field path, following a power line parallel to the downs. Continue forward past a settlement of new houses to the road at Trott, and then turn left.

Do explore this fine village, right down to the crossing by The George, before going along Wrotham Water Road from Miller's Farm (near the pond). It is ¾ mile along this road to Wrotham Water itself, where you should turn right for your car.

Historical Notes

Wrotham (pronounced Rootam) owns a medley of cottages, shops, and public houses – timber-clad, tile hung, and brick – in its two main thoroughfares, High Street and St Mary's Road. It is surprisingly unmolested by noise from the nearby M20 and A20, as they sweep past along the northern boundary. If you venture to the western end of High Street, you will see a fine example of a Kentish oasthouse, still with its cowl, and not obviously pierced with windows, as many now are.

Two 'passageways' give the church of St George a special interest: the unusual arch in the west tower, which may have been part of a processional route and, inside, the Nuns' Gallery high up within the chancel arch. This gallery was probably used not by nuns but, according to one suggestion, by observers keeping a watchful eye on relics and valuables through its tiny peepholes.

Like Otford and Charing, Wrotham once had its own palace, built by one archbishop, demolished by another. Only a vestige remains adjoining 'The Old Palace', a large private house in Bull Lane.

The Coldrum Long Barrow: More commonly known as the Coldrum Stones, this barrow is one of a number of Neolithic burial sites dotted around the hills on each side of the Medway Valley. Four massive stones remain upright. They consist of hardened sandstone left behind by the retreating Ice Age. In 1910 the remains of 22 Stone Age people were found here, and put on display in Trottiscliffe church. The site is owned by the National Trust.

Trottiscliffe: The most memorable aspect of Trottiscliffe (pronounced Trosley) must be the beautiful setting of church, manor house, cottages and farm, in view on the circular walk. Among the church's possessions is a pulpit originally installed at Westminster Abbey. It seems to have been in the way during preparations for George IV's coronation, and was given to Trottiscliffe without formal approval, although this was granted later. The communion rail is unusual in that it has a small alms box embedded into the woodwork (notice the coin slot); and behind the rail are two fine Charles II-style chairs, well secured I might add! These and other 'treasures' are detailed in an attractive leaflet available from the church.

The village itself is ½ mile from the church. It is a typical Kentish village with old cottages, oast houses, and a pond. I should mention that the well known artist Graham Sutherland lived here in the village.

Snodland to Detling

Introduction: Since it is no longer possible to cross the river Medway at Snodland, today's route follows instead the railway line south-wards to the lovely old village of Aylesford, and crosses the river there. The attractive Blue Circle Lakes, the massive Reed's paper factory and Aylesford Carmelite Priory give interest and variety to this semi-industrial scene. The Pilgrims' Way is picked up north-east of Aylesford by the A229 and pursued as far as Detling. The first mile or so is disturbed by the activities of occasional motorcyclists, espe-cially at weekends, and by a short piece of busy road.

The circular walk takes avoiding action by starting just north of Boxley, returning from Detling along a lower route through a pleasant orchard estate.

Circular Walk: Boxley – Detling – Harpole Farm – Boxley
the walk is 2½ miles (4 km) and begins at **(19)** on page 94, just north of Boxley. Car parking is available beside the waterworks near the Pilgrims' Way path (grid reference 774594) where the walk begins.

Pilgrims' Route: Snodland to Detling
The walk is 7½ miles (12 km) and begins at Snodland railway station. There is roadside parking nearby in Church Field.

To return to Snodland by public transport, buses run hourly to Maidstone Mon–Sat (331/334) and 2 hourly Sun (833). A train service operates from Maidstone West, ½ hourly Mon–Sat, hourly on Sunday.

The Walk: From Snodland's railway station turn right into High Street so that the level crossing and parish church are behind you, and follow the road round to the left. Don't cross the main road here (A228) but go forward into Brook Street. **(18)** At the end of Brook Street, just before it joins the A228, turn half-left into the narrow road (not East Street) between industrial buildings. This road crosses

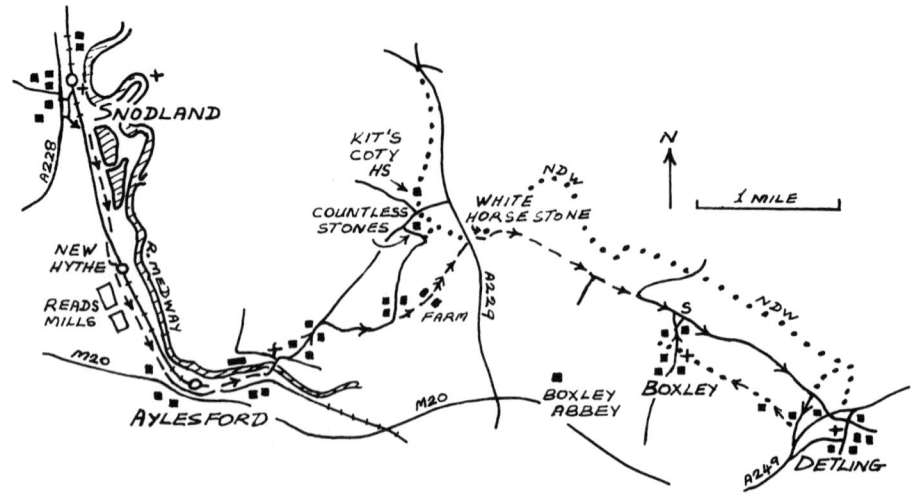

a stream and terminates at a car park. Go under the railway to the Blue Circle Lake and turn right to follow the path between lake and railway.

This first ¼ mile long lake is followed by another, and the path becomes more and more overgrown. Fortunately a wide parallel path beside the second lake makes the going easier. With the lakes behind you the path continues between fences and crosses the railway (take care – it is a frequent service!). The path diverges from the railway line, and joins a wide cul-de-sac. Turn left at the end of this, and right into a path just prior to the level crossing at New Hythe Station. This fenced path runs between the railway and the great Reeds paper mills to the road adjacent to the M20 motorway. Go forward in the road and over a level crossing just beyond Aylesford railway station. When the road (Mill Hall) from the crossing soon curves left, go right to join a path along the river bank.

The impressive and beautiful buildings of Aylesford Priory on the opposite bank relieve this otherwise industrial scene. The quay and adjoining steps remind us of the importance of river transport in earlier days. The Pilgrims' Hall close to the quay is the guests' dining room and is probably the oldest part of the priory.

Just before the old river bridge there is a patch of grass, a seat and a much photographed view of Aylesford. Cross the bridge, turn right into High Street, and left into Rochester Road. Passing the old almshouses on the left, go up to the top of the hill where the fields start and turn right into a road signposted to Pratling Street. After passing a cherry orchard Safeways' massive storage depot dominates the view.

Where the road narrows 100 yards beyond Old Mill Lane branch right along a rough track, passing gardens on the left (including a very superior pigeon palace!) Then everything is nice again, as you come up to Great Cossington Farm. Go straight on through the farm to an iron gate directly ahead, pass to the left of an old walled garden, and bear right towards a stile in the top corner of a field. Looking back you have a good view of the Medway Valley.

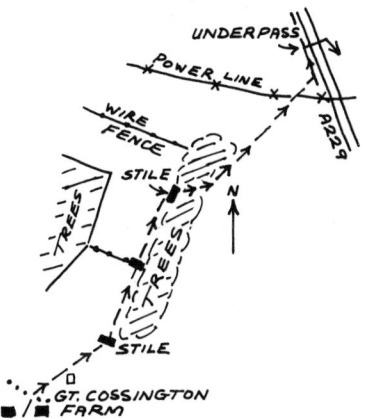

From the stile a terraced path runs forward under ash trees and joins another stile at the far right-hand corner of the field. Go over a stile under trees half-way along the right-hand edge of the next field. The path soon emerges from the far side of the wood and continues uphill along the left edge of a field, meeting a road about 20 yards to the left of a pylon.

At the time of writing the preferred route of the Channel Tunnel rail link places the railway line in an east–west direction 200 yards south of the road. With any luck your path will not be affected to any great extent as it crosses the portal of a tunnel. This tunnel will take the railway under the A229.

Turn left in the road and go along to an underpass (A229). The

Countless Stones (see Historical Notes) are in view to the left of the third electricity pylon in the Medway direction (285 degrees). If you wish to see these more closely – also Kit's Coty House – retreat to a gate on the left and walk the level ½ mile path (the North Downs Way) to a road junction. The two sites are clearly signposted at this point: Kit's Coty steeply uphill; the Countless Stones ('Little' Kit's Coty) downhill. A total round trip of 1½ miles – or thereabouts.

To continue the walk go through the underpass to a service station on the A229, then along a short tarmac drive to the left of a car dealer's. This drive soon joins the Pilgrims' Way which, mercifully, leads away from the noise and clamour.

The White Horse Stone can be seen in a clearing on the left quite soon (see Historical Notes). Forty yards after this the North Downs Way branches left to ascend the downs. The Pilgrims' Way is straight on – for one mile to a hairpin bend in a busy road. As well as the sound of motorcycles you may also hear nightingales hereabouts – as I have!

Go forward on the level in this road for ¼ mile – with great care and on the grass verge! When the road turns right for Boxley, continue straight on into a lesser road signposted to Detling. Then all is peace and quiet again!

(19) Straight on along this most pleasant road (a right turn into it if on the circular walk) for one mile to The Larches, a semi-wooded area on the left. This, as the notice board points out, is a Site of Special Scientific Interest 'principally because of the great variety of plants and other wild life to be found in the chalk grassland'. Unfortunately, 75 per cent of the mature beech trees on this 60 acre site were blown down in the 1987 October storm. If you are on the circular walk turn right into Harpole Lane quite soon, then continue from next paragraph.

To complete the linear walk go straight on to the A249. Cross the A249 to a road opposite, and follow this past Detling village hall to a T-junction by the Cock Horse.

Returning to Boxley From Detling: Go down Harpole Lane for ¼ mile and turn right through an iron gate just beyond a stone tile-hung house, East Lodge. From the gate follow a tarmac drive that serves Harpole Farm. Beyond the farm, the drive becomes a track and soon passes an open barn. It then runs with a line of tall trees, and in due course to the right of a cherry orchard. When the track turns half left, go straight on to a stile and gate; then along the left edge of a field to a stile in its far left-hand corner.

You will soon be following Boxley's churchyard wall, at the end of which a stile connects with The Green. A right turn at the road ahead (by the Kings Arms) will take you back to the start of the walk near the waterworks.

Historical Notes

Snodland has three valued possessions, a 15th century timber-framed Wealden Cottage in High Street, west of the A228, Woodlands Farm further west along the same street, and the old parish church near the railway station.

The arguments for and against Snodland as the point from which pilgrims crossed the river Medway are many and varied, as are those for and against Cuxton, Aylesford and Halling, the other short-listed settlements. In favour of Snodland there are, in Hilaire Belloc's words: 'a number of converging arguments . . . though each is individually slight, the whole bundle is convincing'. For the layman a glance at a map of the area (1 : 50,000 for example) provides proof enough, since Snodland is in line with the Pilgrims' Way both east and west of the river. Large scale maps tell a different story by showing the Pilgrims' Way running north–south on both sides of the Medway valley, destined for a crossing at Cuxton. Although roadside signs 'confirm' this route, they may well be adding error to error!

Aylesford: So close to Medway industry, to 'M' and 'A' roads, yet so much apart, Aylesford retains its delightful old-world appearance. The view from the south bank of the Medway is particularly striking: the medieval bridge, the terrace of attractive houses on the north bank, the fine tower of the parish church – complementing each other in a memorable setting. Another good view, in content more of the 20th century, is to be enjoyed from a path just below the church.

The church itself you will doubtless find locked. Not so the Friars, Aylesford's Carmelite priory, which is open to guests and visitors all the year round. The Carmelite order traces its origins back to a small community living on Mount Carmel in the Holy Land. They came to England in 1242, a small party settling here at Aylesford.

95

Kit's Coty House: An intriguing name (origin uncertain) given to an assembly of three upright sarsen stones topped by a horizontal capstone. It is all that is left of a prehistoric burial mound dating back 4,000 years. This dolmen stands in a prominent position overlooking the Medway Valley.

The Countless Stones: A fallen heap of stones that once formed the infrastructure of an earth-covered burial mound. No research is required into the origin of its name – simply that the half-buried stones cannot be counted with any precision!

The White Horse Stone: A large sarsen stone which may mark the site of a prehistoric burial chamber. It stands a few yards from the Pilgrims' Way. Look at it end on and you will detect in its undulations a certain similarity to a horse's head!

Boxley: A pleasant village but afflicted by constant through traffic. The church is attractively situated at the head of The Green. It possesses an unusual narthex – a single storey porch attached to the west face of the tower. It is possible that this was used for the display of relics.

Boxley Abbey lies one mile south-west of the village (not on our route), and is now a private house. History has recorded the abbey as a 'holy place' where miraculous images were shown to pilgrims – in particular the Rood of Grace. The Rood was a cleverly designed Crucifix with 'a head that bowed, mouth that opened and eyes that rolled'. These movements were performed through the medium of wires and sticks rather than divine intervention.

Detling to Harrietsham

Introduction: From Detling the Pilgrims' Way is one of the best of Kent's country lanes – a continuous uninterrupted walk through the little settlements of Thurnham and Broad Street. Beyond the lovely village of Hollingbourne the lane becomes a straight track between cultivated fields and under trees.

The circular walk from Hollingbourne involves doubling back from a point above Harrietsham station and making the return journey along the Greenway. A most enjoyable way home!

Circular Walk: Hollingbourne – Harrietsham – Greenway – Hollingbourne
The walk is 5 miles (8 km) and starts at **(20)** on page 99, at Hollingbourne War Memorial. There is car parking in the layby just opposite.

Pilgrims' Route: Detling to Harrietsham
The walk is 7 miles (11.3 km). The walk begins at Detling High Street. There is parking here opposite the post office and at the Village Hall.

To return to Detling by public transport, a train service runs to Maidstone East, ½ hourly Mon–Sat and hourly on Sunday. Buses then operate to Detling hourly Mon–Sat, 2 hourly Sun (331/334).

The Walk: The clearly marked Pilgrims' Way leaves the top end of Detling's High Street opposite the Cock Horse. This is the start of an uneventful one mile of quiet road to another horse – the Black Horse – at Thurnham crossroads. If you have time, there are two worthwhile excursions from the crossroads: a left turn and steeply uphill to Thurnham 'Castle'; a right turn for the parish church (see Historical Notes).

To continue on the Pilgrims' Way go straight on from the crossroads, passing Thurnham Friars on the right immediately – an interesting old house with a mixture of building styles. There is another crossing after ⅔ mile, with Water Lane clearly marked on

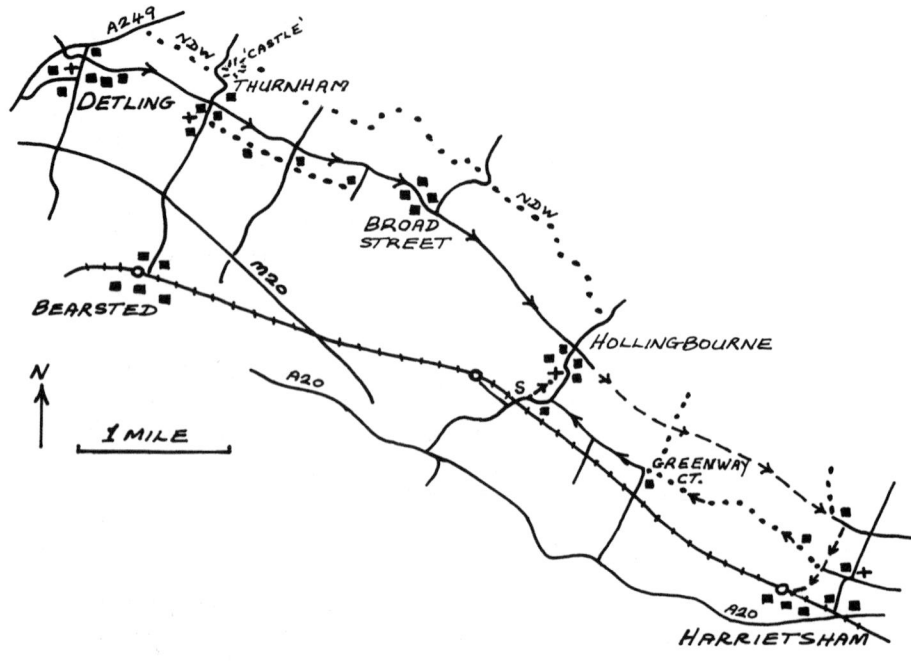

the right. Not a randomly chosen name, but an indication to early travellers that water could be found here.

Forward again to another crossing after ½ mile, passing a 'no through road' on the right. Then another ½ mile into Broad Street. It is disturbing to see so much 'prairy' farming with forlorn roadside stiles facing vast expanses of ploughed earth and seemingly leading nowhere.

Straight on through Broad Street by Charity Barn and Charity Farmhouse, Brushing's Farmhouse and Brushing's Cottage; and ignoring a road coming down from Hucking. Then past Allington Farm (and its little brother) and into Hollingbourne by the Pilgrims' Rest.

For Harrietsham cross the Pilgrims' Way (no through road) opposite, but not before having a closer look at Hollingbourne! **(21)** After the tarmac wears thin and the 'road' turns left, go forward along a track between fields. There is little to be said for the next 2 miles except keep straight on! This means ignoring a wide crossing track and anything else that might tempt you away from the straight and narrow, including a path running parallel on the right as you approach a timber-framed house (Dutch House).

When you reach the entrance gate to Dutch House, if you are staying on the Pilgrims' Way continue from **(22)** on page 101.

If bound for Harrietsham, or for Hollingbourne on the circular walk, turn right into a beech-lined track. For the circular walk continue from next paragraph.

To complete the linear walk go over a drive and continue straight on across fields and alongside a hedge to a stile. Turn right here for the station and for Harrietsham.

Returning to Hollingbourne from Harrietsham: Where the trees terminate, turn right into a metalled drive and head towards Court Lodge Farm, clearly identified by two large hoppers. On passing through the farm the drive becomes a track. Beyond a dip in the fields ahead it turns briefly south (25 yards) to meet an upcoming footpath, and then resumes its former direction along a field-edge, also now as a footpath. Duck under trees in the far left-hand corner of the field; pass an impressively deep combe and, later, enjoy an equally impressive view from a footpath gate (a good spot for a lunch-break!) before continuing forward to join a road beyond Greenway Court. Go straight on in this road (Greenway Court Road) to its junction with the B2163. Turn left for your car or the railway station.

Joining the circular walk from Hollingbourne railway station: From the station's very long approach road go left along the B2163 and under the railway arch. **(20)** Leave the road just beyond Hollingbourne's war memorial and go along a path across fields to the church. From the north side of the church join the road again and follow this up through the village to the Pilgrims' Rest. Turn right here into the Pilgrims' Way and continue from **(21)** on page 98.

Historical Notes

Detling: Another village mercifully relieved of its through traffic. This is a mixed blessing, since the same traffic now roars past the severed end of High Street – out of sight but not out of mind! Where the noise is loudest a venerable Tudor red brick gateway overlooks the narrow Pilgrims' Way from the grounds of East Court – a mansion demolished many years ago. The church stands at the quiet end of the village. It boasts a fine old yew tree outside and a beautifully carved lectern inside. The lectern is all of 600 years old and may have come from nearby Boxley Abbey.

Thurnham: The 'Castle' may be explored by taking the steep road up from Thurnham crossroads. Go forward into a footpath where the road turns sharp left; the 'green castle' extends over a large area to the left of the path. It is steeply undulating (dangerously so in places) and covered to a large extent by a tangle of trees and undergrowth. A more civilised approach is by ascending the road still further: a fragment of the castle's flint wall may be seen on the right – and a magnificent view of 'half the world' on the left!

Commentators have attributed the castle to various civilisations – British, Roman, Saxon, Norman. Being so strategic a site, it is likely that they all, in their time, have held sway here.

St Mary's church is worth visiting (downhill from the crossroads) if only to relax on the churchyard seat and to enjoy the sun glancing through tall lime trees. On the north side of the churchyard an interesting headstone commemorates Alfred Mynn, 'one of the fathers of Kent cricket', who died in 1861.

Hollingbourne: Descending East Street from its crossing with the Pilgrims' Way the first building to catch our attention, for one reason or another, is the Pilgrims' Rest, previously known as the King's Head and before that the Pilgrims' Rest! The half-timbered Malt-house stands next door, while the flint-walled village forge, now an antique shop, is on the opposite corner. Where the road begins to curve left, you will see the imposing Elizabethan manor house, apparently haunted by Catherine Howard!

Before the road turns right to resume its previous direction we enter the lovely precincts of Hollingbourne church. A famous 17th century family, the Culpepers, were closely associated with the church. In the chancel a memorial to John, the 1st Lord Culpeper, describes him as a Master of the Rolls and Chancellor of the Exchequer under the Stuart kings. A valued possession of the church is a superb altar cloth ornamented with many different figures of fruit. This was wrought in gold needlework, apparently by the daughters of Lord Culpeper while he was abroad with Charles II. The altar cloth is kept securely locked away, but may be seen by application to the Vicar.

Harrietsham to Charing

Introduction: From the railway station at Harrietsham a good track runs as straight as a die to meet the Pilgrims' Way near Stede Hill. From here the Way is open and airy – stimulating for the soul and feet! When after two miles this quiet road turns south towards Lenham, the Way continues ahead as a gently meandering path for four miles to Charing, a village of great beauty and interest. Since Lenham is well worth visiting, an alternative footpath route is described which will take you down to the village from the Pilgrims' Way.

Circular Walk: Sadly, there is no suitable circular walk for this section.

Pilgrims' Route: Harrietsham to Charing
The walk is 7 miles (11.3 km) and begins at Harrietsham Station. There is car parking in Station Road and West Street.
　　To return to Harrietsham by public transport, there is a ½ hourly train service Mon–Sat, hourly on Sunday.

The Walk: From the 'east-bound' platform at Harrietsham railway station (the one on which you alight if coming from London) join the footpath that runs parallel to the line. This path soon turns left and heads straight and true for the downs, mostly as a wide track and crossing the Greenway at the half-way point. The Pilgrims' Way is met beside the entrance to Dutch House. Turn right here and **(22)** go ahead to the road at Stede Hill. Once you have crossed the road there is a view of Stede Court and its clock tower uphill on the left.
　　After ½ mile a road comes in from the right and the extensive Marley Works begin to dominate the view. And who hasn't heard of Marley Tiles? Continue straight on from the Marley works and when, after another ½ mile, the road turns right and heads downhill, go forward into a green track. Before the next ½ mile is over the track is

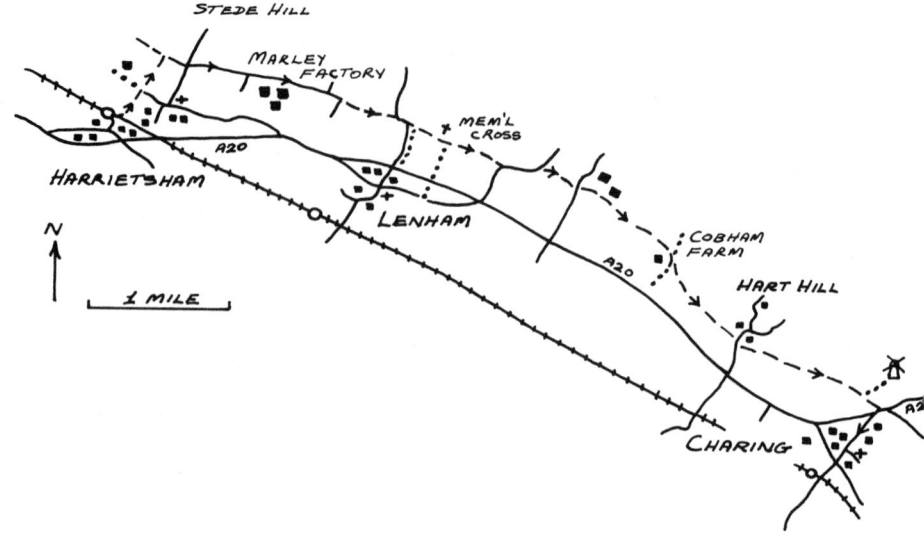

joined by a road coming in from the left. When this soon turns right
for Lenham continue straight on in the tarmaced Pilgrims' Way. (For
a footpath diversion to Lenham see page 103).

You will shortly come to a wooden gate where a drive leads off to
'The House by the Cross'. Straight on again, but now along a wide
greensward. The white cross on the left was cut in memory of those
who fell in the two World Wars. The fine panoramic view from the
memorial seat includes Lenham and its church.

Continue along the wide greensward to a wooden gate and then
along a path under trees. Go left and uphill in the road ahead, passing
a disused quarry on the left. At the far end of the quarry where the
road rises more steeply, branch half right into a narrow path between
hedges. Before long the path runs into a drive serving a row of houses
and meets a road by Lenham's old Chest Hospital. Cross the road to
the track opposite and when after ¾ mile this emerges from hedge-
rows (now as a narrow path), cut across a field to the left-hand side of
a large metal barn at Cobham Farm.

Join the farm track and follow it for a short distance until it turns
right by the farmhouse. Then leave the track for a level route across a
field in the direction of a clump of trees. This will place the farmhouse
behind you and maintain your previous direction. If the path is

102

smothered by rape, keep close to the dividing line between upper and lower fields! From a gate at the far end of the field, it is ¾ mile of level path to the road at Hart Hill Farm, with a crossing track at the half-way point. Numerous sarsen stones decorate the route, possibly moved here from adjacent cultivated fields.

Turn right into the road and go downhill for 40 yards to a path on the left. It is now 1¼ miles of clear path to a house called Twyford – just above Charing. Assuming a good measure of strength and enthusiasm, a short but very steep path 50 yards before Twyford will take you up to the windmill on Charing Hill. This smock mill was built around 1840 and ceased working in about 1892. Sadly, its sails and machinery have gone.

For the through route to Wye, go forward to the A252 and cross this to the Pilgrims' Way, then continue from**(23)** on page 105. For Charing turn right at Twyford, cross the A252 and go down The Hill to High Street.

Footpath route from the Pilgrims' Way to Lenham: Go through a gate opposite a house called Highdown and follow the field-edge round to the right, descending the field until you join a path running between a fence and the road. When you emerge from the path cross the A20 and go forward into Lenham. Return the same way to rejoin the Pilgrims' Way.

Historical Notes

Harrietsham is cut through the middle by the east–west thrust of the A20, a road once carrying a huge volume of traffic but now relieved by the M20 motorway. If you are coming from the railway station you will need to cross the A20 in order to visit the picturesque East Street. Here you will find a formal terrace of almshouses (built in 1642, rebuilt in 1770) and one of the best surviving Wealden houses in Kent, the Old House. This dates from the 16th century and has an outward appearance unchanged since the day it was built – or so it would seem.

The parish church lies on the Greenway, half-way between the village and the Pilgrims' Way, and is noted for having two towers, one 15th century, the other possibly late Saxon. The church is not on our chosen route but can be visited by diverting from the path that is used to reach the Pilgrims' Way from the railway station.

The Marley Factory has come a long way since Owen Aisher set up business in the 1920s making and selling concrete roofing tiles: from a wooden shed measuring 20 ft by 15 ft, to a site covering 65 acres; from a Winget handpress costing £30, to a manufacturing plant worth millions. Today the site is known as the Lenham Complex, consisting of Marley Extrusions (drainpipes etc), Marley Foam for the motoring industry, and (more familiar to you and me) Marley Floors.

Lenham's 'Bright little market square' is ½ mile from the Pilgrims' Way and is so delightful that it is worth sacrificing an hour or so from your day to see it. Among Lenham's outstanding buildings is the Saxon Warriors Chemist in the Market Square, 16th century Forge House near the parish church, and half-timbered Honywood House in High Street.

The chemist shop gained its unusual name following the discovery of a Saxon grave beneath the building in 1946. Honywood House is situated between the Square and the railway station. It is clearly dated 1621.

The parish church contains a very ornate and highly acclaimed oak pulpit, interesting choir stools, and wall paintings which may date from the 14th century. In the churchyard the grave of 46 REME soldiers killed locally by a flying bomb in 1944 is a sad reminder of the Second World War. Before you leave the churchyard, notice the magnificent tithe barn south of the church. And before you leave Lenham, see the 'Lock-up' in Faversham Road. This was originally the mortuary for the village workhouse!

Charing to Wye

Introduction: A magnificent walk linking two of the most attractive and interesting of Kent's villages. And if that is not enough, there is the idyllic setting of Eastwell church and Eastwell Lake, and the typically English village green at Boughton Lees. Beyond Boughton Lees a two mile diversion from the Pilgrims' Way is followed in order to end the day at Wye.

The circular route leaves the Pilgrims' Way at Dunn Street, returning to Charing along country lanes from Westwell to Pett Place.

Circular Walk: Charing – Westwell – Pett Place – Charing
The walk is 6½ miles (10.5 km) and starts at Charing Station. There is a car park in Station Road.

Pilgrims' Route: Charing to Wye
The walk is 7½ miles (12 km) and, like the circular walk, begins at Charing Station.

To return to Charing by public transport trains run ½ hourly Mon–Sat, hourly on Sunday.

The Walk: From Charing railway station go forward to Station Road and over the A20 to join High Street. High Street runs into The Hill, which in turn takes you up to the A252. Turn right in this and then first right into Pilgrims' Way. **(23)** Where a lane comes in from the right there is a good view of Pett Place (at the end of the lane) and, later, Charing church. The South Downs can be seen on the distant horizon (weather permitting, of course!)

At Burnt House Cottage, one mile or so from Charing, the Way turns left and, after a few yards, right, to pass disued lime kilns and an active quarry. Go straight on along what is now a rough track under trees, ignoring a less used branch leaving from the left after 75 yards. The track evolves into a leafy path below Westwell Downs,

105

with a view over Ashford to the power station and its pylons at Dungeness on the south coast.

Beyond cottages 'Wychling Over' and 'Pilgrims Cottage' the Way is tarmaced and the left branch (straight on) at a fork meets a lane coming in from the right. Go forward with the lane for ½ mile to a T-junction at Dunn Street. Turn right for the circular walk, and continue from page 108.

In theory, the Pilgrims' Way continues straight on from here across Eastwell Park, and enters the woodland ahead. This part of the Way is on private land (the longest continuous stretch to be so affected), and has virtually disappeared from the ground. We must follow instead a right-of-way running parallel to it. Go over the two stiles ahead (North Downs Way) and cross a cultivated field to a third stile at the far side – to the right of an open barn. Turn right from that third stile to follow a wide track between fields.

After ⅔ mile an uncompromising 'Private Grounds, Keep Out' notice will confront you so you must turn right here, to follow a fenced wood on the left. After 60 yards turn left, with the wood and its fence still on your left. The tower of Eastwell church should be coming into view ahead, as you make your way forward to a stile and

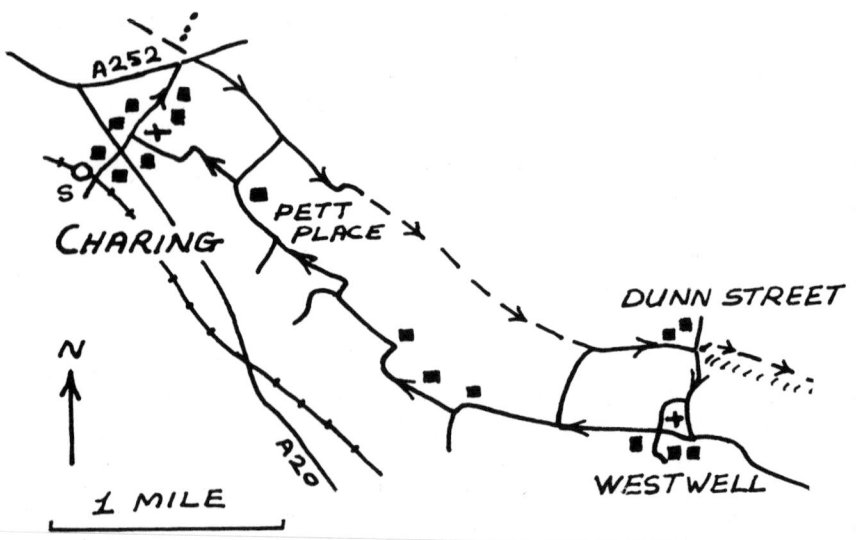

across a cultivated field. Once across the field go forward in a drive from a T-junction, passing to the left of the church. To visit the church and the lake, divert through a kissing-gate on the right.

Back on the drive go uphill towards an ugly tank at the top. The left arm of the T-junction here leads to Eastwell Manor, now a hotel and restaurant; the right arm to the distant, very ornate, entrance gate. I suspect that the line of the Pilgrims' Way is detectable as a slight ridge running from the woods in a direct line towards the Manor. But I may be wrong!

Go straight on from the T-junction, through a kissing-gate and along a pasture, with a tree-lined drive running parallel down on the left. Three-quarters of the way along this pasture (ignore an earlier waymark post) go half left and downhill to a kissing-gate leading onto the drive. Walk along the drive a few yards, then through a gate on the left and into another pasture. Cross this diagonally to a gate in its furthest corner – aiming for the left end of a brick wall. A few more steps and you are on the A251 road at Boughton Lees.

Turn left here and join the right-hand branch of a Y-junction almost immediately. The common will then be on your left. A typical English green, with picturesque cottages, a pub, cricket in action perhaps, and seats to rest those tiring limbs!

Go straight on from the crossroads just beyond Old Forge House into a lane which calls itself Pilgrims' Way. Here begins orchard country, with apples, pears and runner beans! A little beyond a No Through Road on the left (½ mile from Boughton Lees) there is a feature occurring only once – a three-way North Downs Way junction, marked by the usual concrete plinths. For the through route on to Chilham etc, take the left-hand branch through the orchard and

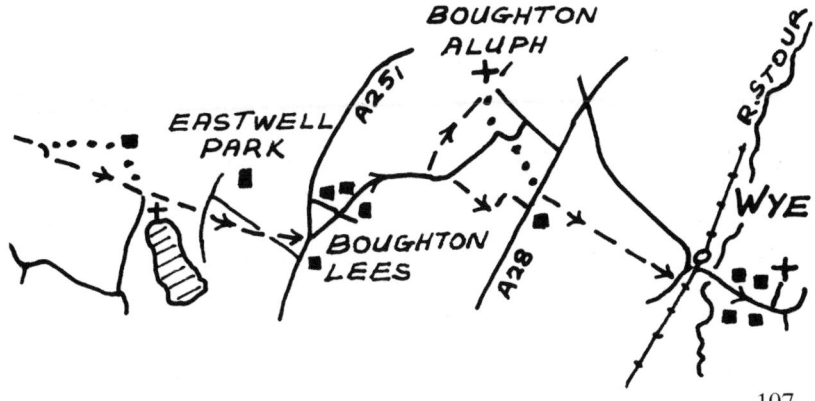

follow the path for ½ mile to Boughton Aluph church; then continue from **(24)** on page 112.

To end the walk at Wye stay in the lane. When the lane soon curves left before a house called Sunridge, go over a stile on the right and follow a field-edge, with the lane on the left, into a corner. Turn right from the corner to follow farm buildings and a tall hedge and orchard left. The lane will now be behind you. At the end of this hedge (a shelter-belt) turn left along the extremity of the orchard. After 100 yards, at a further corner of the orchard, turn right across a large cultivated field towards a marker post on the far side, with buildings beyond.

As you cross the field you will see a crown on the hillside directly ahead. This was cut in 1902 by students of Wye Agricultural College to commemorate the coronation of King Edward VII. From the marker post turn left and follow the hedge for 60 yards to a stile. Cross the A28 here to another stile in a very tall hawthorn hedge opposite. Over that stile and you are in Perry Court Fruit Farm, where (if it's Autumn) you should try not to be too distracted by the delicious fruit on all sides!

As you make your way straight on through the orchard (as directed by acorn waymarks) you may notice that the apple trees are each producing two varieties of 'eaters'. Continue forward at a farm crossing, with buildings right and 'cookers' left. When the 'cookers' come to an end go right for 25 yards and then left. Wye and its church, and the crown on the hillside, are in view ahead as you make your way between strawberries, leeks, cabbages, sweetcorn and marrows to a stile in the hedge at the far end of the farm.

Go straight on now across fields to a cattle grid and a road. Turn left for Wye station. For the village centre cross the river bridge (notice the old watermill on the right) and walk the road for ½ mile to Church Street and its welcoming teashops.

Returning to Charing from Dunn Street: Going downhill from Dunn Street, ignore the first turning on the right and continue past the mill pond to the road junction at Westwell. Turn right here to pass the mill itself – still in a good state of preservation – and the church (still locked, I imagine!). At the crossroad continue forward, with your back to the Wheel Inn, and stay in this straight piece of road for one mile to where it turns left by a tile-hung house. Turn right at a junction almost immediately and follow the road past Digge Court through a succession of right and left turns, passing Lacton Manor and Wooton Manor Farm in the process.

At a junction ahead keep straight on past Pett Place. This grand house in 'plum coloured brick with vivid red dressings' is early 18th century with later additions – three 19th century Dutch gables.

Curve right after Pett Place then forward again from a road junction into Pett Lane. Join a path on the left just before the first of Charing's houses. Turn right with this path after 100 yards and head towards a recreation ground. Cross this to a metalled path between houses, then through the churchyard to Charing's Market Place.

Historical Notes

Charing: It is not easy to believe that this modest village was once home to archbishops and host to kings. If we have, like Donald Maxwell in *The Pilgrims' Way in Kent*, 'imagination well supplied' we may yet 'hear the trampling of horsemen, the welcome of a hundred trumpets, and the clatter and laughter of a great cavalcade'. In the real world, all that is left of the 13th century archbishop's palace is little more than the ruined gatehouse and the once-impressive banqueting hall, now a barn. Imagine Henry VIII dining there!

Overlooking the ruin is the fine buttressed tower of the parish church. It has been said that the block on which John the Baptist lost his head was kept here in the church until the Dissolution of the Monasteries, after which it disappeared. Still remaining in the church is the 'vamping horn', one of only five left in the country. Quite what its function was, no one knows. To accompany the church orchestra, or the choir before the advent of church organs? To amplify the voice of the choir leader? Perhaps all of these!

Among the many fine houses in High Street are Georgian Ludwell House and Wakely House; also timber-framed Peirce House, dated about 1530 and set back from the street.

Eastwell: The longest single stretch of the Pilgrims' Way to be barred to public use lies within Eastwell Park. This is not all bad, since the alternative route takes us close to St Mary's church and Eastwell Lake, a place and an experience not to be missed by any modern pilgrim. The church is a ruin, due to poor construction and war damage by a Second World War flying bomb, and the lake a haven for wildlife.

In 1968 a number of tombs were removed from the church to the Victoria and Albert Museum. Another tomb, unmarked, is reputed to be that of Richard Plantagenet, son of Richard III.

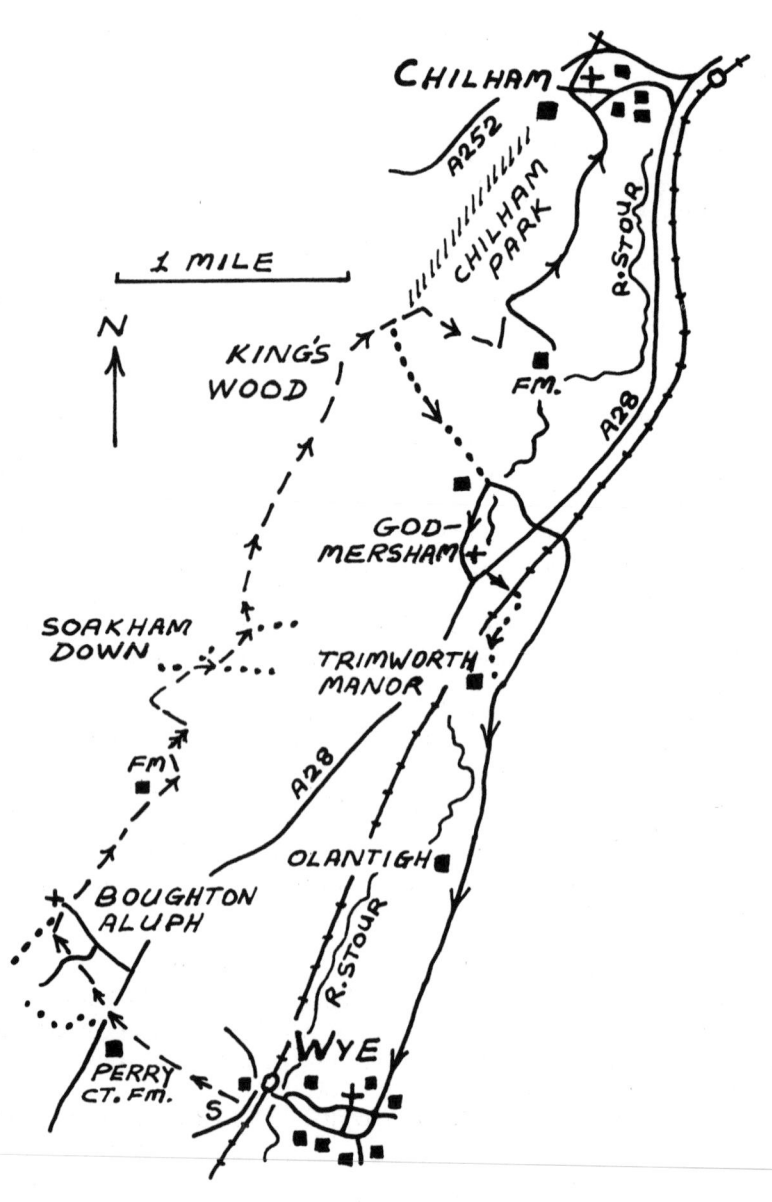

CHILHAM

A252

CHILHAM PARK

R. STOUR

A28

FM.

1 MILE

N

KING'S WOOD

GOD-
MERSHAM

SOAKHAM DOWN

TRIMWORTH MANOR

FM

A28

OLANTIGH

R. STOUR

BOUGHTON ALUPH

WYE

PERRY CT. FM.

S

Wye to Chilham

Introduction: The two mile link from Wye to the Pilgrims' Way at Boughton Aluph passes through the fruitful fields and orchards of Perry Court Farm. From Boughton Aluph the Way soon makes for the heights of Soakham Down, staying at this level for two miles through lovely Kings Wood. Within a mile of Chilham the path turns right and descends to a lower level, joining a quiet road to the village.

The circular walk makes its descent earlier, heading for the delightful settlement of Godmersham, beautifully situated by the river Stour. From Godmersham there is a choice between returning by bus or walking back to Wye, the latter by footpath and road – a quiet road save for the occasional fast motorist!

Circular Walk: Wye – Boughton Aluph – Kings Wood – Godmersham – Olantigh – Wye
The walk is 8½ miles (13.7 km) and begins at Wye Station. There is a car park in Churchfield Way.

Pilgrims' Route: Wye to Chilham
The walk is 6½ miles (10.5 km) and also begins at Wye Station.

To return to Wye by public transport, there is an hourly train service daily. There is also a bus service via Godmersham hourly Mon–Sat only (400/402).

The Walk: From Wye railway station go over the level crossing and turn left immediately at the T-junction. After 100 yards leave the road at a cattle grid on the right and cross three fields in succession at right-angles to the road. From the far side of the third field go over a stile in the hedge and into the grounds of Perry Court Farm. Continue forward between fruit and vegetable plots and alongside a wind-break of young alder trees. Turn right at the end of the wind-break, then left after 25 yards to resume your forward direction.

At a T-junction in a farm drive (the barns and farm shop in view on the left) enter the orchard ahead, as directed by an acorn waymark. Then follow the left side of a wind-break to a stile in a tall hawthorn hedge, near the farm shop entrance.

After crossing the A28 to the stile opposite you should have sight of Boughton Aluph church, the next port of call. If the prospect of treading the intervening field, be it ploughed or muddy, is too daunting, you could go right in the road then first left for the church. Otherwise go half-right from the stile in the direction of a yellow waymark post – to the left of an old rusty barn. On arrival at that post a stile will place you in a lane. Go forward in the lane to where it turns left and cross another good stile on the right.

With a house on the left initially continue forward across two fields in succession, following the waymark posts. After the second field go half-right in a meadow towards the church and join a lane near its entrance gate.

(24) Do enter the church if you have time; you will find it most interesting. It is thought that pilgrims rested here and warmed themselves at a large fire-place in the south porch. The porch remains but no longer provides access to the church.

From the lower churchyard gate, cross the lane to a field and aim for a gate in its far left-hand corner, passing old and new barns on the left. From the gate a path takes you between fences and down into a valley. The ascent on the far side is followed by a left, then a right turn to join a lane at Whitehill Farm.

Cross the lane and follow a track down to derelict Soakham farmhouse. Forward from the farm then soon left between fields to a corner under the hillside. Then right from the corner and uphill in a sunken path towards the trees. Turn left through a gate beside the trees and continue uphill to the summit (Soakham Down). The path turns right at the summit and runs just inside the wood.

Now you must keep your wits about you – I didn't when I first came this way, and became hopelessly lost! After about 300 yards (that's 400 man-size paces) from the last right-hand turn, go half-right at a junction of paths, in accordance with an acorn waymark. This well trodden path runs due east (90 degrees) and soon passes a tall hornbeam tree. Then after a mere 60 yards fork **left**, not straight on. There was once a Pilgrims' Way sign at this point, but now only the supports remain.

Much of the woodland here is planted with sweet chestnut trees

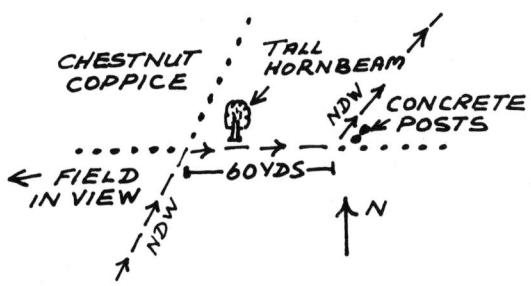

which are cut (coppiced) every 12 years or so for use as fencing pales, hop poles, gates etc. When the path drops downhill to a crossing of ways with a very wide path leaving from the left, continue straight on for just 50 yards, and no more! At this point branch half-left into an uphill path running between a chestnut coppice on the left and a beechwood on the right. The presence of a concrete North Downs Way plinth a few yards along this path will confirm the correct course.

You now have 1½ miles of woodland path going almost straight and level as far as a large Forestry Commission sign 'Kings Wood'. This stretch is punctuated by two paths coming in from the left (ignore these) and gaps in the trees on the right – the first giving a good view of Godmersham Park. A few yards beyond the Forestry Commission sign a stile on the right beside a low brick wall is the turn-off point for the circular route. For this continue from page 114.

The Pilgrims' Way originally continued straight on from here, finally descending through Chilham Park estate. However, except for the first few hundred yards, this part of the route no longer enjoys a public right of access. It is therefore necessary to leave the original Pilgrims' Way and join a lower route to Chilham.

From the Forestry Commission notice go forward a few yards and branch right (not straight on) along a curving path that runs just inside the wood, with a sheep pasture in view on the right. The path soon resumes its forward direction and meets a T-junction.

Turn right here down a good path which soon comes out into the open, while descending steeply. After ⅓ mile it makes an abrupt left-hand turn and gives us a fine view of Hurst Farm with its oast houses, and the surrounding countryside. The path passes under an avenue of beech trees and meets the terminating point of a tarmac road where a private drive heads off to Hurst Farm.

I need say no more, except that it is a very pleasant one mile into Chilham along this quiet road.

Returning to Wye from Kings Wood: From that stile near the Forestry Commission notice board cross a succession of sheep pastures in the direction of a distant radio mast (170 degrees). The route is well marked with yellow pointers and posts. These will guide you downhill to join a farm track adjacent to the right-hand end of a stand of tall beech trees. Go straight on downhill in this wide flinty track, with Godmersham Park (the house) half-right. Pass a farmhouse on the left, and go over a crossing-track.

Turn right from the end of the track you have been following and head towards the gatehouse of Godmersham Park. A small gate in an iron fence will lead you across a well manicured green to the entrance drive and a left turn will see you through the main gate and onto the public road. Turn right in the road (not over the river bridge) and follow this through to Godmersham church. Go left with the road here, and down to the A28. Save 2½ miles now, by catching the hourly bus back to Wye (route 400/402 Mon–Sat only). There are bus stops about ¼ mile in both directions along the A28.

To continue the walk back to Wye go left along the A28 a short distance and over the river bridge. Then immediately cross the road to a stile opposite. The path leaves the road at right angles, crosses a stream, and passes under a railway arch. And here we have a difficulty: the stile on the right just beyond the railway arch and the path into which it leads has become grossly overgrown for some time. Until the path is cleared the best alternative is to walk the edge of the field parallel to the path and the railway, making for a gap and a yellow waymark post slightly left of the far corner.

Cross a drive leading to a house on the right, and proceed along the right-hand edge of a field to a gate beside the barns at Trimworth Manor. Turn left into a track and right when this meets a road. Now it is straight on for Wye, turning neither left nor right along this 2 mile stretch.

At the half-way point you will pass the impressive entrance gates of Olantigh Towers. The equally impressive portico of this 'intensely Edwardian place' is in view along the drive.

Finally, do be careful along this road, and keep to the pavement where it exists. Not many cars use the road but those that do seem to be hell-bent on something!

Historical Notes

From Wye we make contact with the Pilgrims' Way at Boughton Aluph church. From the church the way proceeds north-east for one mile and then goes into an unusually sharp left-hand turn. This was almost certainly to avoid crossing a ravine below Soakham Down. It also placed the route firmly on the ridge of the down, where it remained for 2½ miles before descending to Chilham. The last mile into Chilham is on private land within Chilham Park, and a small part can be explored when the grounds are open to the public (Tues–Thurs, June to August).

Wye: It is a pleasant and interesting ½ mile from Wye railway station along Bridge Street to the centre of the 'town', with the river Stour, the old mill and mill house and the Tickled Trout Inn at one end, and an attractive collection of cottages at the other. Church Street with its Georgian houses and shops is at the centre of things, and links Bridge Street to the church of St Gregory and St Martin and the buildings of Wye Agricultural College.

Those parts of the college nearest the church date back to the time of Cardinal Archbishop John Kempe, a native of Wye who founded here a Secular College of Priests and a free grammar school in 1447. When in 1545 Henry VIII's Commissioners seized the college, the King stipulated that the grammar school should be maintained by whoever in future owned the property. In this way the school continued in existence for more than 300 years until the 1880s. The agricultural college came into being in 1894 and has grown in size and importance ever since. Its reputation is worldwide, with students coming from over 40 countries to study or undertake research in agriculture, horticulture, land use and management, and in related natural and social sciences.

Godmersham: First to come into view as we descend the downs on the circular walk is Godmersham Park. This handsome house was built in 1732 for Thomas Brodnax. In order to inherit two fortunes, Brodnax changed his name twice, and with the proceeds paid for the house. Sounds a good idea!

Jane Austen knew Godmersham well, her brother Edward having once owned the house. Jane was a frequent visitor during the years 1794 to 1813 and wrote parts of her novels there.

The return route takes us along a quiet road from the House to the church of St Lawrence. Flint walls and russet tiles make the church a most agreeable sight, especially in the evening sun. Inside this light and airy church, the 12th century bas-relief of St Thomas Becket is of great interest. Since few representations of the martyr escaped the attentions of Henry VIII's 'destroyers', it is lucky to have survived. It is also interesting to note that the church is still lit, at least in part, by wax candles!

Chilham to Canterbury

Introduction: This final walk along the Pilgrims' Way will be remembered as much for the countryside through which it passes, as for the village of Chilham or the city of Canterbury. Large areas of this undulating countryside are planted with well tended orchards, especially attractive when the trees are in blossom or when the fruit is ripe.

In contrast, the circular walk passes through 'hop country', and along a lakeside nature trail to the outstandingly beautiful Chilham Mill.

Circular Walk: Chilham – Old Wives' Lees – Chartham – Chilham
The walk is 6½ miles (10.5 km) and begins in Chilham Village Square. There is a car park near the fire station.

Pilgrims' Route: Chilham to Canterbury
The walk is 7 miles (11.3 km) and also begins in the Square at Chilham.

To return to Chilham by public transport, there is an hourly train service from Canterbury West. There is also a bus service hourly Mon–Sat only (400/402).

The Walk: From the square at Chilham go down Church Hill to the left of the White Horse, then cross the A252 into the lane opposite, signposted to Selling. At the next crossing continue straight on towards Old Wives' Lees. If you are wondering how this strange name came about, you are not alone, for no one has yet provided a satisfactory answer!

At Old Wives' Lees crossroad, not far from the Star Inn, go half right into clearly marked Pilgrims' Way, soon passing the village hall and the post office. Just beyond the converted oast houses 'North Court Oast' on the left, branch half left into a side road. For the time being you have left the Pilgrims' Way, which makes its way south-east

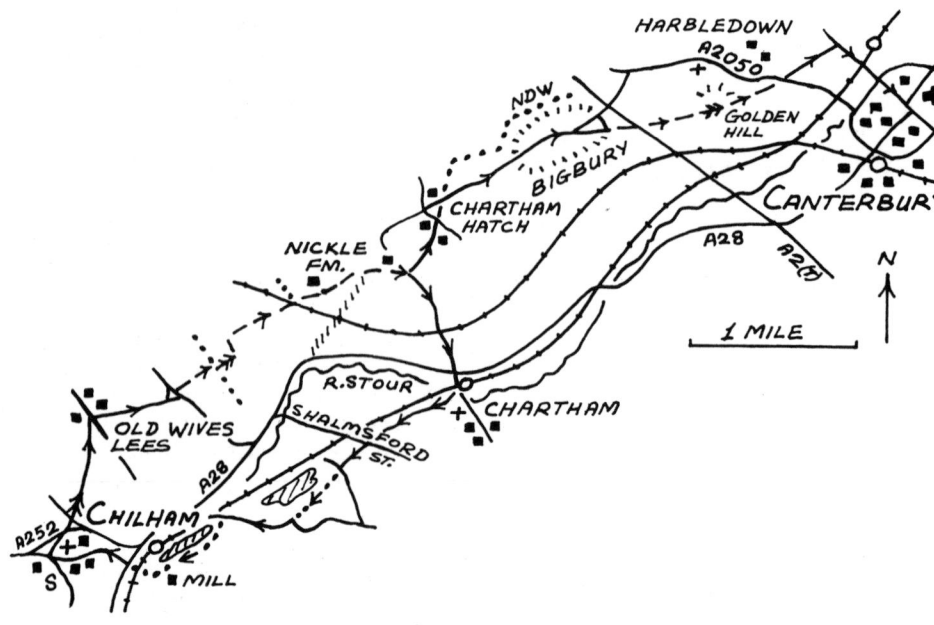

to meet the A28. You would find this unacceptably busy! The short
side road terminates at a T-junction. Turn right here, then left over a
stile after a few yards.

Next through a tunnel of poplar trees, a shelter belt protecting the
adjacent fruit farm. Then downhill between a wood (being felled)
and an orchard to a track at the bottom of a valley. Turn right in the
track and left after 40 yards into a very steep uphill path beside a
magnificent stand of beech trees. A tall hedgerow takes over from the
beech and leads you to a waymark post in a field corner.

Turn left from the corner and follow the field edge (there's an
orchard on the right) to a stile on the right just before the summit of
the field. Over the stile and there is a fine view of oast houses and
orchards – with a heavy, mouth-watering crop when in season!

The path heads towards the furthest left of the oast houses, and
becomes a downhill service track through the orchard. When this
bears right along the far side of the valley cross the railway line by
going over two stiles which may be hidden by Arnolds Fruit Farm
packing cases! Once over the railway turn right immediately and,
after a few yards, join a circulating tarmac drive. Go forward in this

(passing an electricity pole) and downhill through soft fruit planta-
tions to where unconverted oast houses are situated.

Cross the farm drive well to the right of the oast houses and go
steeply uphill, eventually meeting a concrete drive, turning left in this
before curving right on level ground. Then passing a house on the
right, still in orchard country, before arriving at a Y-junction. The
left branch is the continuation of the drive, and follows the power
lines. Your route is the right-hand branch (a rough drive) in the
direction of oast houses and an aerial mast. This leads past Hatch
Farmhouses (closely so, as directed by acorn waymarks), then past
the oast houses of Hopper's Farmhouse Bakery where the 'Cakes of
Kent' smell really good! If you are on the circular walk, turn right in
the road by the bakery then continue from page 120.

To continue the walk to Canterbury turn left in the road by the
bakery and right after a few yards into New Town Street. This will
take you into Chartham Hatch. When in the village the road turns left
beyond a T-junction, go forward along a narrow path to the left of
Nightingale Close and follow this through to Bigberry Road.

A right turn into Bigberry Road and you are on what is almost
certainly the line of the Pilgrims' Way. The North Downs Way takes
a different route from here and avoids more than a mile of road; but
since we are pilgrims good and true we stay in the road – a quiet,
pleasant road, as it happens!

The road passes through the site of Iron Age Bigbury Camp. This
was excavated between 1861 and 1895 when mainly domestic and
agricultural 'finds' were unearthed. This doesn't square with the
suggestion that the 'camp' (or 'fort') was the scene of a battle
between Caesar's forces and the native population in 54 BC. A
portion of the earthen ramparts can be seen by diverting 40 yards
along a public footpath. This path leaves from a stile on the left just
beyond an S-bend in the road less than one mile from Chartham
Hatch.

As you approach a fork in the road there are views of the river
Stour and the suburbs of Canterbury. Go straight on at the fork into a
No Through Road labelled Pilgrims' Way, soon passing a superior
establishment on the left – 'Caesars Grove'.

Given good visibility you should at long last have sight of Canterbury Cathedral directly in line with the road.

At a T-junction just beyond Pilgrims' Cottage turn left, then right
into a track after a few yards. This maintains your direction and takes
you down to the A2(T). Great care is required as you cross this to a

stile opposite, where you are joined by the North Downs Way. Depending on the state of the ground, choose from two paths going forward; then downhill alongside a poplar shelter belt. There is dwarf apple stock on the right, and a view of Golden Hill ahead. Then cross a stream at the bottom of the valley.

After climbing out of the valley you have an opportunity to divert onto Golden Hill, where the grass in Autumn is indeed golden. There is at least one seat here – and a magnificent view of orchard country. This 2½ acre hilltop was given to the National Trust in 1928, primarily as a play area for chidlren, but it is a delight to all!

Back on the path, this changes to a tarmac drive and passes a house called Mill in the Mint. The drive is Mill Lane and leads to a roundabout on the A2050 (previously the A2). Cross to London Road and follow this through to its junction with St Dunstan's Street. For the cathedral take a right turn into St Dunstan's Street to the Westgate (but first see Historical Notes). Then go straight on through pedestrianised St Peter's Street and High Street, followed by a left turn into St Margaret's Street.

Since we left the door of Winchester Cathedral we have walked some 130 miles to reach the great cathedral at Canterbury. Our pilgrimage is over!

Returning to Chilham from Hopper's Farmhouse Bakery: From the bakery turn right in the road and go downhill and over the railway line to the A28. Continue straight on to a level-crossing at Chartham Station, followed by a right turn immediately after the crossing. After passing attractive (and entertaining) Bedford House, Parish Road will take you over the river and eventually beside an old mill, where hops are dried and bagged. Then ascend Bolts Hill to the Cross Keys public house and the crossroads at Shalmsford Street with its post office and foodstore. Go straight on from the crossing for ¼ mile to a T-junction in the road.

Straight on again, but now along a good path across fields, passing what I take to be a one-time hop-pickers' enclosure on the right at the T-junction. In view from the path are the oast houses that we passed earlier at Arnolds Fruit Farm (360 degrees); also Old Wives' Lees (300 degrees); and a flooded gravel pit beside the river Stour, largely hidden by trees.

The path joins a lane by Pickelden Cottage. Go forward in the lane and stay with it when it curves right at Pickelden Farmhouse. After passing a large pond on the right continue forward to a kissing-gate.

This is on the left just after the lane crosses the river Stour, and is the entrance to a path owned by the Mid-Kent Water Company. Although this path is not a right-of-way, it is open to the public daily from 7 am until sunset, and suits our purpose nicely.

This excellent path runs between river and lake for ½ mile before joining the drive to Chilham Mill. Turn left in the drive to see this fine building. Returning from the mill go along the drive to the level-crossing and the A28. Cross the A28 to the road opposite, soon passing the police station on the right. Curve left with the road very soon (not joining the A252 Chilham bypass) and follow it up to the Y-junction by Chilham's Woolpack Inn. Branch right into The Street and continue uphill to the village square.

Historical Notes

There are two possible routes for the Pilgrims' Way out of Chilham. The first is confirmed by roadsigns and goes north to the hilltop village of Old Wives' Lees, then east to join the A28 at Shalmsford Street. The second route arrives at the same point by way of the Stour Valley (A28). At a sharp bend in the river ½ mile north-west of Shalmsford Street, the combined route climbs to Nickle Farm and Chartham Hatch. Why pilgrims should choose the hilltop route, no one quite knows. We choose it because the alternative is entirely along a busy main road.

After Chartham Hatch the Way passes through Iron Age Bigbury Camp. From the camp there are alternative routes for the final run into Canterbury: straight on via Golden Hill, or north-east to join Watling Street through the village of Harbledown. We take the former, more direct route.

Chilham: You will not need me to extol the exceptional beauty of Chilham: it speaks for itself! The Square and adjoining streets, with their timber-frame houses and shops, are a source of pleasure to many, as is evident from the size of the car park!

The stone tower of St Mary's church, with its fine clock dating from 1727, faces the square. Inside there is much of interest, as explained in the helpfully illustrated church guidebook. Included is a memorial to two small sons of Charles Hardy, one-time owner of Chilham Castle. The children, who died in 1858, are shown reading a copy of *Babes in the Wood*. Close to the memorial in the north transept (far left-hand corner) lies a stone coffin. This was opened in 1948 'with great care and formality' in the belief that it might contain the remains of St Augustine. The only items found were records of previous openings – in 1914, 1904 and 1883.

On the opposite side of the square is the entrance gate to Chilham Park. The attractive gardens are open to the public daily, providing an opportunity to conjecture on the route of the Pilgrims' Way through the estate. It seems that the Way emerges in the farmyard, passes along the rear entrance drive and down a no longer used drive to Taylors Hill.

The keep of Chilham Castle is a prominent landmark in the grounds. Constructed in Norman times, the castle was largely dismantled around 1542 and the materials used in the building of Shurland Castle on the Isle of Sheppey. Also in the grounds, and open to the public (Tues–Thurs, June–August), is the red-brick Jacobean mansion.

Photography or wildlife enthusiasts should not let the day pass without a visit to **Chilham Mill and Lake** near the end of the circular walk. The mill is situated on the river Stour ½ mile from the village.

Chilham Lake, a flooded gravel pit between the river Stour and the railway, is next to the mill. The Kent Trust for Nature Conservation (PO Box 29, Maidstone, ME124 1YH) have devised an interesting nature trail around the entire lake.

Canterbury: Having walked all the way from Chilham the last thing you will want is a tour of Canterbury, at least not until you have gathered up your strength! Better to relax in the beautifully kept riverside gardens just south of the Westgate.

Westgate was rebuilt in about 1380 and is the only city gate remaining from the original eight. For 400 years until 1829 it served as the city gaol. It is now a museum – with a good view of Canterbury from the roof. Back on your feet you will doubtless be aiming for the city centre and the cathedral. For this go into St Peter's Street from Westgate. On the left overlooking a branch of the river Stour are the picturesque Weavers' Houses, with a replica of a ducking stool suspended above the water. A little further along the street, on the right, is Eastbridge Hospital, founded in about 1180 as a lodging-place for poor pilgrims. Enter freely (but not for lodging!) through the low Gothic door.

In Stour Street on the right you will find the Poor Priests' Hospital. This was founded in 1220 (and rebuilt in 1373) for 'poor priests disabled by age or infirmity', and now houses the Canterbury Heritage, a fascinating 'time-walk' through the 'spectacle and splendour of Canterbury's story'. Less informative but more amusing (and more expensive!) is the Canterbury Pilgrims' Way, a vivid re-enactment of Chaucer's *Canterbury Tales*. This is located in a medieval church in St Margaret's Street.

Back in the main street (now High Street) and crossing over to narrow Mercery Lane, the jeweller's shop on the corner is part of the original Chequers of the Hope Inn where Chaucer's 29 pilgrims slept on arrival in Canterbury.

Proceeding along Mercery Lane you will soon enter the Buttermarket, a delightful square overlooked by the elaborate Christchurch Gateway. Through the gateway and you are in the precincts of the cathedral, close to the south-west porch.

You may wish to make your own way through the cathedral, and gather your own impressions of this great House of God. There is a waymarked route (you will be familiar with these by now!) that you could follow, however. This will take you down to what is perhaps the most beautiful part of the cathedral, the Norman crypt.

The spot where Archbishop Thomas Becket was murdered in 1170 can be seen in the north-west transept (roughly in the centre of the cathedral). His body lay in the crypt for 50 years until moved to a magnificent shrine in the Trinity Chapel at the east end of the cathedral. The shrine was destroyed in 1538 by order of King Henry VIII.

The walled War Memorial Gardens to the east of the cathedral provide another opportunity for relaxation before continuing your tour of the city. To visit the ruins of St Augustine's Abbey leave the gardens from the north-east corner and cross Broad Street (a main road) to the Fyndon Gate. Turn right here, then left into Longport. St Augustine was sent to England as a missionary in AD 597 and founded this, his second monastery in Canterbury, in about AD 602. It was largely destroyed along with Becket's shrine in 1538. Although there is an admission charge, the ruins can, in part, be seen from the road.

Returning to Broad Street, there is now an excellent short walk southwards along the city wall, culminating in a fine view of the Dane John Gardens and Dane John itself – a huge mound thought to be a 1st century (AD) burial place.

More information about Canterbury is available from the excellent Visitor Centre in St Margaret's Street which is also the starting-point of conducted tours of the city.

Appendix

Buses and Trains

Some useful bus and train links with towns and villages along the Pilgrims' Way.

Only those routes with an hourly service or better from Monday to Saturday are mentioned. On Saturdays the 'last bus' may run surprisingly early, and on Sundays there may be no service at all!
Bus services are subject to change at short notice so please check on routes and times before setting out.

Winchester: Trains from London (Waterloo), Southampton and Poole. Bus 214/215*.
Alresford: Bus 214/215*.
Alton and Farnham: Trains from London (Waterloo). Bus 215*.
Puttenham (A31 crossroads): Bus 215*.
Guildford: Trains from London (Waterloo), Reading, Dorking (Deepdene), and Redhill. Bus 215*.

* Alder Valley bus 215 runs from Guildford to Winchester via Puttenham, Farnham, Alton, Four Marks (for Chawton Park Wood), and Alresford. Bus 214 runs from Alresford to Winchester only (via Itchen Abbas). (214/215 is a most useful service; it is well worth sending for the timetable!)

Dorking: Trains from London (Victoria and Waterloo).
Dorking (Deepdene): Trains from Reading, Guildford and Redhill.
Merstham: Trains from London (Victoria) and Oxted.
Westerham Hill: Bus 410 from Redhill, Oxted and Bromley railway stations.
Otford and Kemsing: Trains from London (Victoria) and Ashford, Kent.
Wrotham: Trains from London (Victoria) and Ashford to Borough Green and Wrotham; then one mile walk to Wrotham village.
Snodland and Aylesford: Trains from London (Charing Cross); change at Strood.
Detling: Bus 331–334 (833 Sunday) from Maidstone, Sittingbourne and Faversham.
Hollingbourne, Harrietsham, Lenham, Charing: Trains from London (Victoria) and Ashford. Bus 10 from Maidstone, Ashford and Folkestone.
Wye, Chilham, Chartham and Canterbury West: Trains from London (Charing Cross), Ramsgate and Margate.
Canterbury East: Trains from London (Victoria) and Dover.
Chilham and Wye are also served by bus routes 400–402 from Canterbury (bus station).

ACCOMMODATION

This small selection of addresses is chosen from those offering the most economically priced accommodation. More complete lists are obtainable from the tourist information centres listed below. 'EM' indicates that an evening meal is available. Note that the name of the telephone exchange is given only when it differs from the name of the town or village.

Hampshire

Winchester: Mr D Fletcher, 33 Christchurch Rd, SO23 9SY. Tel: (0962) 65442.

Mrs C Owen, 61 Cheriton Rd, SO22 5AY. Tel: (0962) 53379.

Itchen Stoke: Mrs P Pitt, The Parsonage, SO24 0QU. Tel: Alresford (0962) 732123.

Alresford: Mrs M Read, The Old Manse, East St, SO24 9EQ. Tel: (0962) 734396.

Mrs R Wrigley, Taplins, South Rd, SO24 9HR. Tel: (0962) 732133.

Surrey

Farnham: Mr & Mrs Sievewright, Woodlawn, Swingate Rd, GU9 8JJ. Tel: (0252) 733922. EM.

The Sands: Mrs S Hoyland, Sycamores, Sands Rd, GU10 1LW. Tel: Runfold (02518) 2117.

Guildford: Mrs J Braithwaite, 11 Castle Hill, GU1 3SX. Tel: (0483) 63324. EM.

Shere: Mrs M James, Manor Cottage, GU5 9JE. Tel: (048 641) 2979.

Mrs O Warren, Cherry Trees, Gomshall Lane, GU5 9HE. Tel: (048 641) 2288.

Dorking: The Pilgrim, Station Rd, RH4 1HF. Tel: (0306) 889951. EM (not Sun).

The Waltons, 5 Rose Hill, RH4 2EG. Tel: (0306) 883127. EM.

Oxted: Mrs J Snell, 12 Hoskins Rd, RH8 9HT. Tel: (0883) 712700.

Kent

Westerham: Miss B Myfanwy Davies, Cartref, Croydon Rd, TN16 1TX. Tel: (0959) 63394.

Mrs N Godsal, The Orchard House, Brasted Chart, TN16 1LR (2 miles south of the Pilgrims' Way). Tel: (0959) 63702.

Otford: Mr G Levien, Moat Bungalow, Station Rd, TN14 5QU. Tel: (09 592) 4165.

Detling: Mrs P Wallace, Merville, Pilgrims' Way, ME14 3EX. Tel: Maidstone (0622) 39920.

Hollingbourne: Mrs Taylor, 12 Tile Fields, ME17 1TZ. Tel: Maidstone (0622) 880253.

Harrietsham: Mrs H Atkins, Mannamead, Pilgrims' Way, ME17 1BT. Tel: Maidstone (0622) 859336; EM.

Mrs D Passey, Westmead, West St, ME17 1JD. Tel: Maidstone (0622) 859448.

APPENDIX

Lenham: Ms C Madge, Marley Farmhouse, West St, ME17 2EN. Tel: Maidstone (0622) 858621.
Charing: M Okell, Arketts Farm, TN27 0HH. Tel: (023 371) 2893; EM; no smoking; 1 mile north of the Pilgrims' Way – approach from Hart Hill.
Mrs H Cavell, Broadview, Pluckley Rd, TN27 0AE. Tel: (023 371) 2808.
Wye: Joan & John Morris, Cornercroft, Church St, TN25 6BN. Tel: (0233) 812133.
Boughton Aluph: Mrs B Fearne, Warren Cottage, TN25 4HW. Tel: Challock (023 374) 483.
Chilham: Mrs J Wood, Bagham Cross, CT4 8DU. Tel: Canterbury (0227) 730264.
Canterbury: Acacia Lodge, 39 London Rd, CT2 8LF. Tel: (0227) 769955.
London Guest House, 14 London Rd, CT2 8LR. Tel: (0227) 765860.

Youth Hostels on or close to the Pilgrims' Way include those at Winchester, Tanners Hatch (on Ranmore Common near Dorking), Holmbury St Mary (2 miles south of Abinger Hammer), Kemsing and Canterbury. Membership details are available from the Youth Hostels Association, 8 St Stephen's Hill, St Albans, Herts, AL1 2DY.

Tourist Information Centres   *0420 88448 (Alton) Tourist board*
The Guildhall, The Broadway, Winchester, Hampshire, SO23 9LJ. Tel: (0962) 840500. 10 a.m.   *Buses: 0962-852352*
Locality Office, South St, Farnham, Surrey, GU9 7RN. Tel: Godalming (04868) 4104.
The Civic Hall, London Rd, Guildford, Surrey, GU2 1AA. Tel: (0483) 575857.
Buckhurst Lane, Sevenoaks, Kent, TN13 1LQ. Tel: (0732) 450305.
The Gatehouse, Mill St, Maidstone, Kent, ME15 6YE. Tel: (0622) 602169/ 673581.
Lower High St, Ashford, Kent, TN24 8TE. Tel: (0233) 37311.
34 St Margaret's St, Canterbury, Kent, CT1 2TG. Tel: (0227) 766567.

Alton/um 0252 2332

Bus Company Addresses
(and phone numbers for timetable enquiries)
Routes 10, 400–402*: East Kent Buses, Station Rd, Ashford, Kent, TN23 1PP. Ashford (0843) 581333.
Route 22: Tillingbourne Bus Company, Little Mead, Cranleigh, Surrey, GU6 8ND. Guildford (0483) 276880.
Routes 25/26: Kentish Bus, Apex House, London Rd, Northfleet, Kent, DA11 9PD. Gravesend (0474) 321300.
Routes 214/215/453: Alder Valley, c/o Hampshire Commercials, Mill Lane, Alton, GU34 2QJ. Alton (0420) 83787.
Routes 331–334/833, 400–402*: Maidstone and District, Luton Rd, Chatham, ME5 7LH. Maidstone (0622) 690577.

126

Country + Croston

(handwritten annotations at top of page)
Auster Jon/Feb 11-4.30
Sat: 11-4.30 New Alresford: 8.23 (then 1123)
Sun: 11-4.30 (Sun Hotel)
Sun: /Dec/Mar Wed-Sm Winchester:
Nov/Dec/Mar Apr 1 30ct-daily
£1.50.

Sunday 453
Sat X69
7.48/8.18
8.13/8.43
9.03/9.23
9.18/10.03
X69/69
10.03/10.23
10.18

APPENDIX

Routes 405, 410, 414: London and Country South West, Lesbourne Rd, Reigate, Surrey, RH2 7LE. Reigate (0737) 242411.

* Joint operation.

Taxis Services
Winchester: Taxi ranks, tel: (0962) 52602 & 52867.
Alton: First Choice Cabs, tel: (0420) 541153.
Farnham: Station Taxi Rank, tel: (0252) 716316.
Guildford: Beeline Taxis, tel: (0483) 236666.
Dorking: Grey Cars, tel: (0306) 884528 (not weekends).
Amber Taxis, tel: 886231.
Reigate (near Merstham): Gold's 24 Hour Taxis, tel: (07372) 44051/46240/ 49644.
Merstham: Station Taxi Office (not Sun), tel: (07374) 5588 & mobile (0860) 338836.
Oxted & Westerham: AKM Private Car Hire, tel: Oxted (0883) 715079; Westerham (0959) 61030.
Sevenoaks (near Otford): Beeline Taxis, tel: (0732) 456214.
Dave's Taxis, tel: 458998.
Borough Green (near Wrotham): Borough Green Taxis Service, tel: (0732) 882020.
Maidstone (near Detling): ACM Cars, tel: (0622) 51516.
Hollingbourne: Hollingbourne Hire, tel: Maidstone (0622) 880308.
Canterbury: Buss Taxis, Tel: (0227) 450022/768960.

Eating Out
Winchester: Raffles Tea Room, The Square.
Waltons, The Square.
Spinning Wheel, High St.
Harvest Bakery, High St.
New Alresford: The Tiffin, West St.
Chawton: Casandra's Cup.
Alton: Country Craft, Market Square.
Henry Adlam, Market Square.
Philbeam's Cafe (opposite Gateways).
Farnham: Elphick's, West St.
The Coffee Shop (restaurant), Lion & Lamb Yard.
The Borough Coffee Shop, near the Town Hall.
Seale: Herb's Restaurant & Tearoom, Manor Farm Craft Centre.
Compton: Old Congregational Tea Shop (Wed to Sun only).
Loseley Park: Tearoom in the grounds (Wed–Sat 2–5 pm, June–Sept); no entrance charge.
Guildford: Springle's Restaurant (in Debenham's store).
Pew's Restaurant, Chapel St.

Richaux Coffee House, Friary Centre.
Shere: Aster's Tea Shop, Middle St.
Frederick's Restaurant, Upper St.
Abinger: Clock House Tea Rooms.
Gomshall: Restaurant at the Watermill.
Dorking: Haskett's, South St.
Box Hill: Tea Room at the National Trust Centre.
Merstham: Quality Cafe, Station Approach.
Burford Bridge: Ryka's Cafe.
Oxted: Pat's Pantry, Station Rd East.
Westerham: Tiffin's, The Green.
Market Square Tea Rooms.
Tudor Rose Restaurant, The Green.
Otford: Gossips.
Willow Tea Rooms.
Aylesford: Sherlock's Restaurant, High St.
Horsa Cafe, High St.
Charing: Mullian's Restaurant, High St.
Mardee House Tea Rooms, High St (closed Tues).
Harrietsham: Indian Restaurant, on the A20.
Lenham: Chopsticks and Bowl, High St.
Wye: Wye Hill Restaurant and Tea Room, Church St.
New Flying Horse, Bridge St.
Chilham: Copper Kettle, The Square.
Tea Room at Chilham Castle.
Canterbury: Becket's Restaurant, St Peter St.
Cathedral Restaurant, Church Gate.
Perrings (furniture store).

In addition to the above there are many public houses serving meals.